D1060102

QUARTERLIFE

QUARTERLIFE

The Search for Self in Early Adulthood

Satya Doyle Byock

RANDOM HOUSE · NEW YORK

Quarterlife is a work of nonfiction. Some names and
identifying details have been changed.

Copyright © 2022 by Satya Doyle Byock

All rights reserved.

Published in the United States by Random House, an imprint
and division of Penguin Random House LLC, New York.

RANDOM HOUSE and the HOUSE colophon are registered trademarks
of Penguin Random House LLC.

Library of Congress Cataloging-in-Publication Data
Names: Byock, Satya Doyle, author.
Title: Quarterlife: the search for self in early adulthood / by Satya Doyle Byock.
Identifiers: LCCN 2021042256 (print) I LCCN 2021042257 (ebook) I
ISBN 9780525511663 (hardcover) I ISBN 9780525511670 (ebook)
Subjects: LCSH: Young adults—Life skills guides. I Quality of life. I
Self-actualization (Psychology)
Classification: LCC HQ799.5 .B95 2022 (print) I
LCC HQ799.5 (ebook) I DDC 646.70084/2—dc23/eng/20211108
LC record available at https://lccn.loc.gov/2021042256
LC ebook record available at https://lccn.loc.gov/2021042257

Printed in Canada on acid-free paper

randomhousebooks.com

2 4 6 8 9 7 5 3 1

First Edition

Book design by Victoria Wong
Book illustrations by Nina Bunjevac

To my parents, Anita, Ira, and Yvonne,
who have modeled living life with passion and integrity.
There's no greater gift.

"What is to come will be created in you and from you. Hence look into yourself. Do not compare, do not measure. No other way is like yours. All other ways deceive and tempt you. You must fulfill the way that is in you."

—CARL JUNG, *The Red Book*

Contents

Author's Note

Each client portrayed in this book is a composite story from my psychotherapy practice. No character represents a single client, and all identifying details have been changed. In a professional field rooted in the sacredness of confidentiality, there are few ethical guidelines on how to capture clients' experiences as case studies. My goal was to offer stories that honor a strict adherence to confidentiality, without oversimplification or a reliance on tropes. I can only hope I have succeeded.

The COVID-19 pandemic is not discussed in this book. Most of the manuscript was written before the virus, when I was still working with clients in a physical office. As it was always my intention for this book to be relatively timeless in its makeup, I chose not to alter the content to reflect recent changes in my psychotherapy practice or in the world. The pandemic has affected the lives of everyone alive today in one way or another, and I have no way of knowing what the world will be like when these pages are finally in readers' hands. And that was always the point: to write this book so that Quarterlifers in any era might read it and find direction.

Introduction

"Why do I feel lost?"

"Why is my life such a mess?"

"Why am I stuck?"

"What's wrong with me?"

I hear it all. From subtle doubts to unrelenting panic, there is undeniable, epidemic suffering among people in their late teens, twenties, and thirties. Crippling anxiety, depression, anguish, and disorientation are effectively the norm. Suicide rates are unspeakably high, as are overdoses. Compounding the problem, the common diagnoses and solutions being offered to those suffering frequently add to the chaos and stress, as if this stage of life has caught individuals and the healthcare system by surprise. It's not just a question of mental illness. At root, there is not a deep understanding of what is unfolding in this time of life. There isn't even public consensus on what to call these twenty years or so following adolescence.

I call this stage "Quarterlife," derived from the term "Quarterlife crisis," originally coined by Abby Wilner in 1997, and on the rise when I was entering adulthood in the early 2000s. Quarterlife is a distinct period of human development in need of its own road map and soulful guidance. It needn't be a time relegated to expectations of cascading crises, familial hand-wringing, and personal shame. Nor should it be a time during which problems are primarily attended to with medical solutions.

This book is about the alternative.

I became a psychotherapist focused on working with people in this stage of adulthood because I lived through disorientation during these years myself. When I went looking for insight and answers about why I felt so emotionally overwhelmed, I found very little information or support. The life that I'd been raised for through years of school did not seem to align with the life I was expected to be living on my own. Like most people in this age group, I was sent up the ladder of academic development: first grade to second grade, fifth grade to sixth, all the way through high school and college. Then I was released into the world as if I'd been trained for a life beyond academia. But I hadn't been. I hadn't been taught how to cook healthy meals or change a tire, let alone how to ask myself who I was or what I wanted out of life. Moreover, I hadn't been offered tools to make sense of living in a world beset by countless overlapping social and environmental catastrophes. As much as my peers and I had been led to believe that life is a tidy, incremental staircase toward certain goals—career advancement, marriage, home ownership—at some point we each discover that it is not. The linear impression of adulthood is based on antiquated, heteronormative gender roles and racial and economic hierarchies that suggest that a fulfilling life can be achieved through the checking of boxes. It can't be.

Quarterlife is not a sterile journey. It demands the gathering of *experiences*—messy, embodied, uncharted experiences. Full psychological development cannot be accomplished without complex relationships, failures, risks, longings, and adventure. Indeed, despite Western culture's desire to mitigate mess and chaos, psychological development in Quarterlife doesn't follow a simple plan. Experience is the basis of finding one's own life, a life that, by nature of it being entirely unique, does not have its own map or clearly defined path. As the mythologist Joseph Campbell said when reflecting on the journey of life: "If there is a path, it is someone else's."

But there are common patterns that can serve as guideposts along the way.

The chapters that follow will offer some insight into the timeless journey of Quarterlife, first through exploring some historical depictions of this time of life in literature and memoir, and then through the stories of four clients from my psychotherapy practice: Mira, Conner, Grace, and Danny. These stories, beginning in Part II, will model how four very different Quarterlifers learn about themselves and start to find their way.

Understanding this time of life begins with identifying the two types of Quarterlifers, their goals, and what I call the four pillars of growth. I'll present "Meaning Types" and their search for stability through the stories of Grace and Danny, and "Stability Types" and their search for meaning through the journeys of Mira and Conner. Whether you're a Quarter-lifer primarily in search of meaning, or one primarily in search of stability, the ultimate goal is to have both—an experience of wholeness and ease within one's own life.

The four pillars of growth are like wayposts of development: Separate, Listen, Build, and Integrate. These are not linear stages or tasks to be accomplished, but areas of important psychological work in Quarterlife that can lead to significant shifts in well-being and satisfaction. This work requires both receptivity and dedication. It is not easily accomplished, and there are countless structural, systemic obstacles that add to the difficulty and disorientation. And yet, remarkable transformation, even from egregious traumas and suffering, can happen, and knowing some of the patterns of development can help.

This work does not need to happen in therapy, but therapy provides a safe, consistent place for deep contemplation and embodied healing, guidance, and an opportunity for self-reflection that is rarely found elsewhere in the modern world.

Countering widespread admonishment against self-involvement in Quarterlife, I encourage my clients to take an interest in their own lives and experiences—past, present, and future. I emphasize expansive curiosity versus the search for finite conclusions. All of this self-interest helps to ease depression and anxiety in the short- and long-term, and uncover the very individual path through life that one seeks. Quarterlifers have typically imbibed a whole host of contradictory messages around how to be an adult: namely, to be functional and successful, but also popular and attractive; wealthy and famous, intelligent and interesting, creative and entrepreneurial, but not self-involved or selfish, nor privileged or cruel or unaware of the world's pain. In order to abide by these competing implicit and explicit directions—none of which are about genuine self-knowledge or self-care—Quarterlifers can become profoundly disoriented. In contrast, the more that Quarterlifers explore the information of their bodies and histories, their old traumas and stress, and their own points of desire and longing, the more they'll learn to hear what their instincts know about their futures. This is the work I promote. Not patches for one's supposed brokenness, but instead curiosity for how one's own body and soul respond best to the external world, to relationships, intimacy, family history, food, and the varieties of experience within culture and society.

This book is for anyone between the ages of (roughly) sixteen and thirty-six who is desperate to change things about themselves and their circumstances, who is exhausted or scared, depressed or anxious, maybe even hopeless. It's for anyone trying to build an adult life free of endless misery or nagging uncertainty, and one instead filled with clarity, direction, and joy. It's for people trying to find their way on a suffering planet. It's for people reflecting on this time of life in order to gain orientation to where they are now. And it's for the parents, therapists, and educators of Quarterlifers too. The ultimate goal, through self-investigation, is to find and create one's own life and purpose in a complex and deeply fraught world. Despite the popular and oft-repeated derision, this is not "navel gazing." It is the work that the ancients encouraged: "Know thyself and you shall know the gods."

PART I

CHAPTER 1

Something Better Than This

My interest in this time of life began as I neared my college graduation. I couldn't help but notice that practically everyone in my class was uncertain about their future. Except for the calm and happy few who had jobs lined up or were headed to law school, the scene felt like Godzilla had suddenly arrived on our shores. Some people started to panic and were throwing themselves in one direction or another, seeking some plan, any plan, to survive. Some seemed utterly resigned, as if they'd determined that their best days were in the past. Others still were partying a little too maniacally, as if they believed that keeping the college life going would make the enormous threat disappear.

Up until that point, we'd studied, written papers, and taken tests. We'd played sports, protested, partied, eaten lunch together in the cafeteria, and lain out on the vast lawn when it wasn't raining. We were occupied almost all of the time, but we were focused on getting through school and getting to graduation. Each class had deadlines and tests. Each semester led into the next one, until graduation day itself was reached only after a last round of finals and preparation for visiting family. It happened quickly. Suddenly, here we were: finishing nearly two decades of school with very little direction on what to do afterward. Ample attention had been spent on how to get us into college and on sales pitches for which schools to attend, but now we weren't customers anymore, just a bunch of people in our early twenties being tossed from the academic nest with no instruction other than: *Go. Go on. That's all we have for you.*

I felt no clearer about what I was doing with my life than I had in high school. Most of the time when I expressed my existential protestations, they fell on deaf ears. This was just "the way things are," and I would "figure it out." I found myself reflecting on one of the last scenes in the beloved romcom of my youth *Say Anything*. When I was a lovesick teenager, the scene that I'd replay over and over was of Lloyd Dobler holding a boombox above his head, like Romeo wooing his Juliet. (Of course, I also listened to the song he was playing, "In Your Eyes" by Peter Gabriel, on repeat.) But as I neared graduation, another scene from that movie started to creep into my consciousness. Diane Court, class valedictorian and Lloyd's Juliet, delivers a speech to a throng of fellow graduates and parents with whirring video cameras. She says at the end, "I have all the hope and ambition in the world. But when I think about the future, the truth is . . . I am really . . . scared." That was me in a nutshell. All the ambition in the world, and undeniably, utterly scared.

Three years after graduation, I was working as a project manager at a software start-up in downtown Portland. Between this job and college, I'd tried to devote myself to a career in humanitarian work or social justice. I'd applied to countless nonprofit jobs and had volunteered a couple of times abroad, first at a prison in Bogotá, Colombia, and then on the tsunami-ravaged coastline in Sri Lanka. I'd also worked various part-time, entry-level jobs to pay my bills. And in the early days of both "social entrepreneurship" and social media I'd tried to start a company that would connect young people like myself with opportunities to help communities at home and abroad. (Hence the foray into start-ups and tech.) This project manager gig was my first well-paid, full-time job since graduating, and I was grateful to suddenly have a savings account. But I wasn't happy. Beyond financial survival, I was no closer to understanding "the point" of what I was doing, nor did I feel like I was living a life destined for me. I had a "good job" and was grateful for that, but I was helping to build an entirely uninspiring tech product seemingly born from the connections of an old boys' club rather than any genuine vision or need. Most days, I stared out the window at the summer sky from twenty-six floors up wishing that I were on the ground and on my bike instead. I had attempted to create a life for myself that made sense to my insides and also made an impact on the world, but I was failing. This wasn't what I'd envisioned for my future. This couldn't be the purpose of all I'd been working toward in so many years of school.

I spent a lot of time journaling back then and wrote about my perpetual sense of disorientation. I wrote about all the wild animals that seem to have some form of navigation built into their instincts. Like how when male wolves leave their pack and venture into the world, they appear to have a sense of direction and purpose. Or how elephants find water, no matter the distance. Turtles find the gulf streams in the ocean and know when and where to lay their eggs on the beach. Monarch butterflies migrate thousands of miles along the same route. But we humans are going it alone, relying completely on plans, goals, strategy, and blind luck to find our way in life. What happened to our instincts? Despite a comfort with logic in school and the world, that kind of intentional planning had never come easily to me when it was applied to my own life. No matter how much I wrote it down or talked it out, I struggled to understand what the right decisions were, and to hear what my body and feelings were telling me. I had the freedom to roam anywhere, but I usually felt more like a miserable tiger trapped in a cage, pacing back and forth—and a little "too" reactive—than a creature wild and free.

After work one evening, I stepped into the white bungalow I shared with roommates, panting and exhausted from a fast bike ride home in the late summer heat. It had been a rough week. There had been layoffs at my office and the best people around me, many of whom I managed, had suddenly lost their jobs. Meanwhile, all of the most loathsome people had been retained, including the predatory chief executive and his little brother, whose lack of skill radiated off of him like a stench. I knew I had no desire to continue in that environment. I was helping to build a product in which I had no faith, now surrounded by people whom I didn't respect. I was supposed to be filled with the eagerness for life that people expected of someone my age, but I was losing inspiration day by day and losing faith in the life I'd hoped to live. As I began telling my roommates about my day and a conversation with my boss in which he tried to convince me not to quit, I suddenly burst into heaving sobs and collapsed onto the floor. I'd reached my breaking point. I had no idea what I was doing with my life and couldn't, despite advice, stop thinking about it. I felt nauseous from competing beliefs and looming decisions to make: Quit the stupid tech job; wait for the stock options; go back to multiple part-time jobs; take the opportunity for advancement; gain experience; take time off; grow through the pain.

None of it provided clarity about my eventual goal. I knew I wasn't interested in having children, and the idea of marriage still felt a long way away. Was my goal, then, to just accumulate wealth and climb the ranks in a company? No matter where I looked, all I saw were dead ends. I couldn't quiet my mind. I couldn't find my center. I felt totally overwhelmed, exhausted, and also painfully bored by the emptiness of my concerns. Nothing I was doing was making a dent in a world in perpetual crisis. Nothing I was doing was bringing me a clear sense of joy or purpose. Crying on that wooden floor, I felt crazy and stuck. As a college grad and a twenty-something, I was supposed to be thriving. What was wrong with me?

Despite my lack of clarity on almost every front, I started to see patterns in the suffering, or posturing, around me. From my roommates to friends, dates, former classmates, and co-workers, I was surrounded by people more or less my age who were struggling in similar ways. Some of my peers were having a much harder time than I was. Some were in and out of hospitals with complex diagnoses, and some were even on suicide watch. Many others, though, appeared much more stable than I felt. They didn't seem regularly on the brink of sabotaging the very foundations of their life because of existential concerns. They didn't seem plagued by *What does it all mean?* But they also didn't seem entirely certain of what they were doing either. Not only had few of us received lessons on how to handle the myriad things in our independent lives— job hunting, budgeting, taxes, dating, sex, boundaries, cooking, cleaning—but it also seemed like we were supposed to be fine and, in many cases, were being *told to be fine*. Mental health crises, depression, and anxiety seemed sort of hush-hush, while jokes about the supposed shallowness of our generation were on the rise.

Those jokes always struck me as bizarre. Most generations have significant social crises with which to contend, and that helped to shape their worldview. Ours was no different. We were a generation coming of age in the aftermath of 9/11 and the return to endless wars abroad. Climate change increasingly loomed over our future like the most ghoulish apocalypse film ever conceived, and then there were large-scale economic crises to contend with as we attempted to pursue the American Dream. Meanwhile, we were forced to grow accustomed to mass shootings in our schools and in our grocery stores, our concerts, movie theaters, and malls.

It didn't feel like anyone was really looking out for us. The justice system, riddled with racist policies and private interests, had incarcerated countless people my age and younger, seeing criminals where it might instead have seen young citizens in need of tangible support and direction; there were police and courtrooms where there should have been mentors and social aid. Many of my peers were struggling in jobs with wages that couldn't possibly sustain a thriving life; some were living in poverty or homeless. Many of us had crippling student loans and credit card debt accrued, in part due to predatory practices that specifically targeted our age group. Many of us had survived traumas and abuse and had been left without proper psychological or physical care. Many were in and out of drug and alcohol rehab as a result. Too many had died of overdoses, victims of a national epidemic—fueled by corporate greed—that would only grow in coming years. And most of us didn't have reliable health insurance, if we had it at all. Meanwhile, when any of us went to doctors or psychologists for help with our anguish, anxiety, and depression, we were typically given short appointments that concluded with fast diagnoses and prescription drugs. There was rarely much inquiry into *why* we were feeling the way we were, let alone valuable guidance on what to do about it.

As I wept in anguish on the dirty floor of that rental house, I knew there had to be solutions for my lack of direction. I knew there had to be greater meaning behind the confused, neurotic pain that so many of my peers and I felt. I could not believe that we were meant for overcrowded jails, homelessness, gun violence, a list of mental disorders, chronic pain, or endless cycles through treatment centers. If there was an epidemic of suffering among people in my age group, something larger was at play and we were not each individually to blame.

I quit that job, and it felt great. I was sure that it wasn't where I belonged. And while I didn't yet know where I was supposed to be, I did somehow know, as the social psychologist Kenneth Keniston had written years before, that a person "may feel that they have a right to 'something better than this,' without being able to define the 'something.'" I knew there was something better. I just didn't yet understand what or where it was.

Around this time, following one of many emotional phone calls with my patient and worried mother, I received a padded mailer from her with a book inside. The title, *Care of the Soul,* piqued my interest and I read it quickly. Written by a psychotherapist and former Catholic monk, it spoke about orienting to life less cognitively, more through instinct and one's entire being. I asked my mother to point me toward more of the same kind of book and she suggested *Memories, Dreams, Reflections* by the founder of analytical psychology, Carl Jung. I picked up a copy at the bookstore and, once home, sat on my mattress on the floor, the wrinkled maroon covers below me, and devoured that book. I underlined sentences and scratched stars and check marks in the margins. "My whole being was seeking for something still unknown which might confer meaning upon the banality of life." I felt so seen.

It took me years to put into words what was ultimately so important about what I was reading. At the time, all I could tell was that something in this book and these ideas was going to give me direction and change my life. Jung understood humans in a way that resonated deeply with my experience of the world, and in a way that I'd never heard anyone else express. When he wrote about the necessity to find and live one's *own life,* I felt validated in my endless questioning and my search for *more*. More so when he emphasized the pursuit of *wholeness* in life, versus perfection or accomplishment. Sitting with those pages, I felt a deep, enduring sense of calm like I hadn't felt in a long, long time.

As I read more of Jung's work and understood the focus on symbolism and the unconscious, I soon joined a dream group to explore my very frequent dreams. I started therapy with a Jungian analyst, and then, with very little forethought but more clarity than I'd had in years, I began graduate school to study Jungian psychology. I knew two things: I wanted to explore these ideas that had suddenly brought me so much peace, and separately, I needed to learn what the broader field of psychology knew, or thought, about this erratic, confusing time of life.

In graduate school and beyond, I discovered that part of the problem with understanding development in this period of life is how ill-defined this stage between adolescence and midlife has been. In fact, it wasn't until I opened a private psychotherapy practice and started using the term "Quarterlife" that I finally stopped stumbling in my speech, tripping over the various labels that we've come to use for these two decades or so of existence.

The commonly used names for Quarterlife are various modifications of adulthood or adolescence: *extended* adolescence, *young* adulthood, *early* adulthood, or *emerging* adulthood. There are a lot of conflicting perspectives on each of these terms within the psychological literature, but each one implies a state of being *in-between*, as if these twenty-some years of life are merely a transitional zone between other "real" life stages, a sort of lobby you wait in until something important happens. Even worse, the prevailing impression is that adulthood arrives when you finally reach certain markers of economic and relational security, as if those achievements will magically pull you out of the lobby of your suffering and into the grand hall of "real life." All the stages of life prior to Quarterlife have established developmental markers, as well as anticipated periods of stress and struggle. But, unlike the current view of adulthood, those stages are not based on achievements. A toddler who cannot yet form words is no less of a toddler. Equally, a toddler who is learning to play Mozart is not suddenly an adolescent. Though benchmarks of development may be set, prior life stages are not defined by successes or failures. Adulthood shouldn't be either. Modifiers to "adolescence" and "adulthood" too often end up serving as pejoratives.

Another problem in our collective understanding of these years in human development is the common use of whatever generational name is *en vogue* in any given decade. The very practice of generational labeling is tied to the Quarterlife years. As with "millennials" and now with "Gen Zers," generational names are roughly applied to "twentysomethings" (yet another term) as if it describes their stage of life rather than their generation. This is a huge issue that propagates tremendous confusion and misunderstanding. Currently, many millennials are squarely in Quarterlife while others have entered midlife. More Gen Zers are entering Quarterlife every day, while many more are still in adolescence and childhood. The generation and the stage of life are not equivalent.

Nor are all people in one general age group the same. Generational stereotypes are built from outsider opinions and have historically been drawn from the American white middle class to then be projected onto an entire economically and racially diverse group of people in their twenties and thirties. Moreover, these stereotypes seem to serve the primary goal of condescension and ridicule: Older people use them to lament the state of younger people, a long-standing and tiresome trend. "The youth of today is not the youth of twenty years ago," developmental psychologist Erik Erikson wryly observed in 1968. "This much any elderly person would say, at any point in history, and think it was both new and true."

Within developmental and clinical psychology, the absence of an accepted term for this age group is a core problem. It's hard to gauge what's "normal" or "healthy" without proper terminology, and when each generation is studied anew. I use "Quarterlife" to speak about this stage because it's a word free of modifiers or pejoratives, and because it merely denotes a specific period in the arc of existence. Quarterlife begins with indefinite markers, just like all stages of human development. Depending on their lived experience, each person will feel that they've left adolescence and entered Quarterlife somewhere between the ages of sixteen and twenty. They'll then leave Quarterlife for midlife somewhere between thirty-six and forty. Simply put, Quarterlifers are adults between adolescence and midlife. Quarterlife is the first part of adulthood.

We've long needed a developmental understanding of this time of life. Cultures will constantly change, new technologies will enter our lives, and new crises will afflict us. Those things will shape generational experiences, but they won't redefine the foundations of human development and health. We don't have to reinvent the wheel every couple of decades with new statistics on demographics and behavior patterns. When it comes to the timeless practice of becoming human and creating a life for oneself, a changing world is the backdrop, not the story.

CHAPTER 2

The Timeless Search

There is a rich and soulful log of Quarterlifers throughout history and literature who have grappled with the same issues across time, culture, and demographics. Saint Augustine's *Confessions,* published around 1600 years ago, is considered the first Western autobiography, but it might most accurately be described as the first Quarterlife memoir. In it, Saint Augustine—then Aurelius Augustinus Hipponensis—wrote: "I found much to bewilder me in my memories of the long time which had passed since I was nineteen, the age at which I had first begun to search in earnest for truth and wisdom. . . . I realized that I was now thirty years old and was still floundering in the same quagmire." Aurelius was resisting marriage, the pressure of his heavily involved mother, and his own predilections toward obsession with money, fame, and influence. He was deeply preoccupied with finding the right path for his life. Marriage and a successful career seemed easy, but they didn't answer the deeper questions he sought. And in this way, Aurelius wasn't an enigma of his time. He and two close friends felt lost and were searching for answers together. "We were like three hungry mouths, able only to gasp out our needs to one another. . . . We tried to see the reason for our sufferings. But darkness overshadowed us and we turned away asking, 'How long is this to be?' "

I was preoccupied by similar things in college. As I became increasingly overwhelmed with questions about my future, I—like many before me—found *Letters to a Young Poet*. This collection of letters from the great poet Rainer Maria Rilke to a nineteen-year-old, Franz Xaver Kappus, gave me tremendous solace. Kappus had originally written to Rilke in 1902 from his Austrian military academy, a school that Rilke had also attended, with questions about whether he should become a poet and how to live. Rilke replied, "You mustn't be frightened, dear Mr. Kappus. If a sadness rises in front of you, larger than any you have ever seen; if an anxiety, like light and cloud-shadows, moves over your hands and over everything you do. You must realize that something is happening to you, that life has not forgotten you, that it holds you in its hand and will not let you fall."

Seemingly every line of Rilke's letters gave me comfort when I read them in my late teens and for years following. They also gave me some of the earliest hints that my depression and confusion weren't unique to me, or to my time. Rilke was himself just twenty-seven years old when he began writing those letters. He had gained comfort from the work of the Danish author Jens Peter Jacobsen, whose 1880 novel, *Niels Lyhne,* tells the story of a Quarterlifer trying to make his way in the world. Niels's suffering felt familiar to me too. "There must be some defect in him, he would tell himself, some incurable flaw in the innermost marrow of his being, for a human being *could* become whole by living, he did believe that." That's a line that I've read countless times and it still moves me. It encapsulates for me the simultaneous pain and longing that is so core to Quarterlife. Niels Lyhne was frustrated by his own failed attempts to achieve the life he wanted, or to manage life in a world that often overwhelmed him. "These perpetual attempts at a leap that was never leaped had exhausted him, everything was empty and worthless for him, distorted and confused, and so trivial as well." In my own Quarterlife, I'd endured the "attempts at a leap that was never leaped" an infinite number of times and seen it in my peers. I've since seen it over and over with clients too.

Once I started gathering Quarterlife stories from novels, memoirs, and historical records, I began to see the same dissatisfaction and disorientation everywhere. I noticed, for instance, that the anguish of Quarterlife was embedded in the modern feminist movement. In her 1949 magnum opus on women's lives, *The Second Sex,* French philosopher Simone de Beauvoir described the experience of being a young woman anticipating adult life. "It is a painful condition to know one is passive and dependent at the age of hope and ambition, at the age when the will to live and to take a place in the world intensifies; woman learns at this conquering age that no conquest is allowed her, that she must disavow herself, that her future depends on men's good offices." As the Quarterlife years encompass the bulk of female fertility, questions—or certainties—of partnership and childbearing loom large. Gender roles are often stark and restrictive. As de Beauvoir put it, women's natural instincts in Quarterlife toward "hope and ambition" and "the will to live and to take a place in the world" were in direct contradiction to the social expectations of passivity and dependency placed upon them. Their various emotional and physical symptoms were the inevitable result.

American feminist Betty Friedan expanded on this idea in her 1963 book, *The Feminine Mystique,* about the secret malaise that so many American housewives were feeling, though they were expected to be perfectly happy and content. Strangely, my feelings as a college grad forty years later, single and unencumbered, were very similar. I'd done everything that had been expected of me in this era and by my family: a college degree in lieu of marriage and pregnancy. And yet, within that privilege and freedom, I still wondered, as Friedan had put it: *Is this all?* "It was a strange stirring, a sense of dissatisfaction, a yearning that women suffered in the middle of the twentieth century in the United States. . . . As she made the beds, shopped for groceries, matched slipcover material, ate peanut butter sandwiches with her children, chauffeured Cub Scouts and Brownies, lay beside her husband at night—she was afraid to ask even of herself the silent question—'Is this all?' " She'd done everything that had been expected of a Quarterlife woman of her era. She had everything society told her she should want. But she couldn't help but wonder if there wasn't supposed to be more to existence.

For the author Richard Wright, *Is this all?* was an anguished reflection on the entire country in which he'd been raised. Wright's memoir, *Black Boy,* is a largely Quarterlife story about surviving poverty and segregation in America in the early 1900s while struggling to forge a creative life. At twenty years old, having left the Jim Crow South for Chicago, Wright was denied a job as a regular postal clerk because, after a lifetime of chronic malnutrition, he weighed just under what was required for the position. In many ways, he blamed himself. "Waves of self-doubt rose to haunt me. Was I always to hang on the fringes of life?" But he also felt the injustice of losing a career path for which he was fully qualified because "of a few pounds of flesh," and he reflected on his struggle with the "material way of American living that computed everything in terms of the concrete: weight, color, race, fur coats, radios, electric refrigerators, cars, money." Wright longed for something more. He had creative ambitions. He wanted to be a professional writer and had been studying writing on his own for years. Nonetheless, the doubt in his capacity to have that career permeated everything around him. At home, Wright had to grapple further with the doubting inquiries from his aunt Maggie, with whom he, his brother, and his mother lived in close quarters.

My excessive reading puzzled Aunt Maggie; she sensed my fiercely indrawn nature and she did not like it. . . .

"Boy, are you reading for law?" my aunt would demand.

"No."

"Then why are you reading all the time?"

"I like to."

"But what do you get out of it?"

"I get a great deal out of it."

And I knew that my words sounded wild and foolish in my environment, where reading was almost unknown, where the highest item of value was a dime or a dollar, an apartment or a job.

It was something internal that demanded Wright's focus. His "hope and ambition" drove him forward, an aching, desperate urge when he received neither emotional nor tangible help from others.

In movies and television, Quarterlife characters are *everywhere*. Our heartthrobs in rom-coms and heroes in adventure stories are typically Quarterlifers. And yet, these depictions are so common and usually so dramatized that they render the stage of life itself strangely invisible. We observe fantastical stories built on the relative youth of these characters, but we less frequently see honest interpretations of *how hard* this period of life can be. Quarterlife characters are objectified, fetishized, and almost dehumanized as a result.

Meanwhile, Quarterlife is the stage of life most often depicted in global mythology and folk tales, the oral storytelling traditions that entire cultures knew and listened to for entertainment, but also for psychological guidance. The stories that reverberated in young ears expressed explicitly: Life will include ups and downs, some of the downs may almost kill you, but there are ways to survive, strange ways; if you get through the danger and confusion, you will have changed for the better—you'll be you, but grown and transformed. These stories taught something much deeper and more supportive than the modern trope "what doesn't kill you makes you stronger." They taught about the intangible parts of life. They taught about the return of joy, the erotic, the pleasure of existence that is possible after trials of loneliness, pain, terror, and boredom are processed, integrated, and understood. These stories taught young people to trust themselves and to know that life is an obscure, individual journey of meaning wrapped in a tale of social accomplishments and failures.

In the popular Grimms' fairy tale collection alone, stories like "The Three Languages" and "The Story of the Youth Who Went Forth to Learn What Fear Was"—two of my favorites— tell of Quarterlife men being banished from town by their fathers after struggling to find their vocation in life. Each Quarterlifer sets off on a journey filled with catastrophes and confusion, entirely unlike anything they've encountered before. And each finds, in the end, that the solution to their anguish is a far cry from what they might have imagined. These travelers learn that their true pursuit is not about achievement or heroics. In these tales, such inflated desires tend to be thwarted by humiliations and injury. There's a far deeper goal at play.

Stories like these are core to what mythologist Joseph Campbell began to identify in the 1940s as the Hero's Journey theme in global storytelling, a theme that I was grateful to start understanding in my midtwenties. Hero's Journey stories convey the transformation of a person—almost always a Quarterlifer—from one level of consciousness to another. It's a transformation that occurs through some combination of risk-taking, happenstance, hard work, and magic; never through pure logic or planning alone. All of these stories, Campbell wrote, are really about "the maturation of the individual."

Campbell broke down the Hero's Journey structure into three primary stages: Departure, Initiation, and Return. He identified this as the same structure of traditional initiatory rites once hosted by societies worldwide when boys reached puberty and a new stage of psychological life. "The stages of human development are the same today as they were in ancient times," Campbell wrote. "As a child, you are brought up in a world of discipline, of obedience, and you are dependent on others. All this has to be transcended when you come to maturity, *so that you can live not in dependency but with self-responsible authority.*" (Emphasis mine.)

When read symbolically versus literally, mythic stories and fairy tales offer a great deal of insight into what Quarterlife development requires. Within these stories and also tucked away within Jungian psychology—the scholarship that inspired much of Campbell's work and now my own—there is a veritable road map, a system of guideposts to provide psychological orientation for Quarterlifers out in the world alone. And yet, some important updating is required. Most of this past work was based on male development, and myths with male heroes. We are long past the point of needing a Heroine's Journey to counter the Hero's Journey, but instead need a gender-neutral understanding of the possible paths—one more outward and conquering, one more inward and contemplative. The development of consciousness has patterns and pitfalls just as biological development does. But it needn't be gendered. There is a natural course of development, two classic types of Quarterlifers throughout history, and a goal that they all share.

CHAPTER 3

Stability and Meaning

Just as humans get the urge to start crawling and then walking at roughly the same ages, we all long to venture into our own lives around the same time too. Quarterlife is the point at which people traditionally leave their family of origin and begin the work of wrestling themselves into an independent existence. Whether bound initially for work, parenthood, marriage, or school, each person struggles to emerge into the world and into a new life.

However, the journey of Quarterlife is not merely a search for a partner and career, but for oneself. The ultimate goal is for an experience of wholeness: a life that no longer feels like one thing on the inside and another on the outside. The search is for a cessation of the plaguing longing for something *else,* something *more.* Quarterlifers often desire greater security, safety, and social stability, as well as a sense of adventure, experience, and personal meaning. We need sturdy structures for consistency and we need the mystery, intimacy, and even uncertainty that gives life warmth and purpose too. The way

I speak about this in Quarterlife psychology is as the often bewildering longing for *both stability* and for *meaning*.

Adulthood

In the mid twentieth century, as the midlife crisis gained prevalence and attention, large tremors began to disrupt the expected goals of adulthood. In big enough numbers that it began to resonate across societies, midlife adults were suddenly in pursuit of the indefinable "more." The midlife crisis was defined as a point of psychological transformation, a time when adults have to adjust to the "empty nest," when many marriages crumble, and when personal crises, like the deaths of one's parents, trigger existential and spiritual questions. Older adults were no longer expected, across the board, to feel satisfied merely by survival, security, and family. Too many middle-class, midlife adults had woken up to the fact that there was something missing in life, something else they needed.

This earthquake of the midlife epidemic created a chasm in adulthood, which developmental psychology then concretized. The first half of adulthood became the stability stage, emphasizing the goals of economic and personal security, and the propagation of children. The second half of adulthood, midlife and beyond, became the meaning stage: a time to discover oneself through creative work, relationships, and the exploration of the inner world. It's a simple breakdown of adult goals that makes intuitive sense: Create stability before seeking meaning. Root down into life before reflecting too much on existence, spirituality, or mortality.

In practice, however, that clear split of developmental goals for adulthood is rare and unrealistic. It's a model that reflects the course of life for a very specific demographic, and is a narrative that, even in its prime, wasn't true for many populations who felt trapped by the limited expectations of material security and heteronormative goals. Indeed, the countless stories of Quarterlifers that we treasure in history, literature, and myth *are stories* because they don't fit into this simplistic narrative. They weren't able to find stability so easily or they felt empty and stifled by what they'd found. Still, this rubric of adult goals—the smooth development of stability in Quarterlife then the search for meaning in midlife—has long dominated our understanding of adulthood. Like many other long-held cultural beliefs, it begs for reconsideration.

To date, Quarterlifers have protested through their symptoms, crises, creative work, and activism against a narrow depiction of adulthood as defined by capitalistic expectations of achievement and performance; the stifling gender roles of heteronormative patriarchy; and the economic and social abuses of white supremacy. Driven in large part by the vocal discontent of Quarterlifers from all backgrounds over the last century or so, strict gender roles have continued to loosen, labor laws have changed, higher education has become more accessible, birth control has raised the average age of first pregnancy, and the assumed values of adulthood have been subject to further scrutiny. The very idea of sequenced developmental goals—stability first, meaning second—has been thrown into question. The reality is that the search for stability *and* meaning has always been part of Quarterlife, not stability alone.

Today, many Quarterlifers are feeling the loss of those former guardrails of segmented development, and even clear-cut gender roles, while feeling liberated too; there's appreciation for the increased freedom, along with overwhelm and confusion about "the point." The solution is not to regress to the past and so-called "traditional" family roles. The former goals are unsatisfying. But the new goals have yet to be clearly defined.

Ultimately, Quarterlife is about forging one's independence and existence and clarifying, *individually* and *specifically,* what stability and meaning look like. Thriving in Quarterlife does not require being "normal" or "good" or "successful." The longer those narratives persist, forcing people to live lives that are incongruent with their natures or values, the longer an epidemic of concerning mental health statistics will plague Quarterlifers. The more we can see that both stability and meaning are appropriate and healthy inclinations, the less adulthood will be about "winners" and "losers," or "good" and "bad."

Since most developmental psychology has implicitly focused on stability goals in Quarterlife, guided by an assumption that the pursuit of meaning occurs at midlife, we've seen only half the story. In fact, all along, there have been *two types of Quarterlifers*: those who are more inclined to pursue stability first, and are relatively comfortable with that focus, and those who are more inclined to initially pursue meaning, and who have found themselves at odds with the social expectations for this stage of life.

It's a broad spectrum, but I call these two groups, simply, Stability Types and Meaning Types. Understanding these two types of Quarterlifers is the first step to understanding Quarterlife psychology. Once a person clarifies their own place on this spectrum between Meaning Types and Stability Types, they will feel more motivated to tackle everything that Quarterlife requires, rather than feeling overwhelmed by confusing tropes, antiquated expectations, and life advice that may be exactly contrary to what they need.

Meaning Types

There have always been Quarterlifers who have struggled to care about the singular emphasis on gaining stability. In the 1930s, French author Colette Audry journaled about her general reluctance: "I wanted to grow up, but never did I seriously dream of leading the life I saw adults lead. . . . And thus the desire to grow up without ever assuming an adult state, without ever feeling solidarity with parents, mistresses of the house, housewives, or heads of family, was forming in me." Reflecting on Audry's crisis, Simone de Beauvoir explained, "She does not want to remain a child. But the adult world seems frightening or boring to her." What might be referred to today as "extended adolescence" was, for Audry, a conscious choice to dig in her heels to avoid a future that she did not want.

Social psychologist Kenneth Keniston wrote about this avoidance in 1970: "While some young men and women are indeed victims of the psychological malady of 'stretched adolescence,' many others are less impelled by juvenile grandiosity than by a rather accurate analysis of the perils of injustices of the world in which they live." Keniston understood the ambivalence toward adulthood that masses of Quarterlifers in the '60s and '70s were actively and fervently protesting. These Quarterlifers didn't want to live the lives they saw their parents living, or support the world they saw their parents supporting.

Children often feel eager to gain the freedom and independence of adulthood. Adulthood is what an entire childhood seeks to achieve. But when adulthood looks like a wasteland of values, or a place absent of social concern, it may also be rational for Quarterlifers to hesitate to grow up. "Were adult roles viewed as exciting and fulfilling," Keniston wrote, "there could be little problem for most men and women, even the most discriminating, about conforming to the adult world. What makes conformity appear as a danger is that what one conforms to seems so humanly unappealing."

In the era of anti-war protests, civil rights, and second-wave feminism, this fear or reluctance among Quarterlifers to focus on stability values had increased exponentially. But the phenomenon itself wasn't new. There have always been people who found the standard social expectations of adulthood uncomfortable or intolerable, whose inner sense of self was at odds with the external expectations of an adult culture that appeared vacuous, immoral, or just dull.

Historically, these hesitant Quarterlifers have been considered social outcasts: the artists, writers, activists, bachelors, spinsters, dropouts, hysterics, or depressives. Some died young from addiction or mental illness, or were buried away in family histories. A few were lauded as geniuses, but still viewed as exceptions to the rules. In various ways, they've been seen as "failures," and often subjects of shame and sadness for their families.

Each country and culture has their own names for these nonconformists. But for the most part, developmental psychology has neglected to chronicle their existence beyond their symptomatology. They become "sick" in some form, like countless writers, artists, and healers in history, or diagnosed with any variety of disorders. They may often become "criminals" and disappear from society that way. They are categorized according to their diagnosis, record, or addiction and they then vanish from developmental psychology too. There's a lot more going on with these Quarterlifers than the labels suggest. They're Meaning Types, and they don't have to be outsiders.

While Meaning Types can feel ill-equipped to function emotionally or logistically out in the world, internally they may feel older or wiser than their biological age. They're often brimming with genuine aptitude and talent, but struggle with the day-to-day tasks required in modern life. Meaning Types often have negative emotional associations with money and linear time, which can hamper their participation in society. Money is considered gross, dangerous, evil, dirty, or the root of human suffering. Linear time, meanwhile, is "a prison," "a social construction," "a way to keep people chained to capitalism." These associations create an unconscious tension between their often less expressed or acknowledged desires for a full, secure, and stable life.

Meaning Types often long for more ease in life, but they struggle internally against ever becoming "a sellout" or "the walking dead." As a result, many are handcuffed by resentment, and blame the world and its systems for their inability to live full and functional lives. Their struggle is not just to be "functional" or "successful." In addition to logistical difficulties with time and money, there are psychological traps that have to be faced and solved. Meaning Types are more likely to appear emotionally overwhelmed, depressed, caught in intellectual abstractions, or even veering toward psychosis. They may feel linked to a deep sense of mythic time or timelessness. At the far end of the spectrum lie clinical diagnoses like schizophrenia. Meaning Types can feel like they're connected to everything, but struggle to feel singular and differentiated. They may tend to isolate and pull away from others. Sometimes a desire for seemingly endless sleep, isolation, or heightened introversion can be exactly what a person needs to heal, but Meaning Types can also get stuck there, consciously or unconsciously refusing to emerge into the external world.

Meaning Types haven't historically had classic midlife crises, as their life prior can feel like one continuous crisis. If Meaning Types survive to reach midlife, they've often done so because they've figured out how to manage or thrive in the outer world. They found their stability and could combine it with their meaning. Indeed, Meaning Types need to work toward balancing themselves out, seeking a form of stability and functional social living without losing connection to their sense of meaning, even if engaging in such work may feel abhorrent at the outset. I'll explore all of this in more depth in the next chapter, through the stories of two Meaning Type clients from my practice, Grace and Danny.

Stability Types

In contrast, there have always been people who seem to more naturally succeed at "adulting" as prescribed by their culture. The Quarterlifers who tend to appear more successful, healthy, and relatively "put together" I refer to as Stability Types. Where Meaning Types are stereotypically "the artists," philosophers, or musicians, Stability Types are "the lawyers," people in finance and business, and people consciously seeking marriage. These Quarterlifers may prioritize good grades, strong performance in extracurriculars, long-term planning, saving money, maintaining a steady job, pursuing career advancement, and building a family: all of the goals of security once seen as the inherent work of adulthood. They may have strong religious or political perspectives, though they have not yet encountered a lot of doubt or inner struggle with their belief system. If there is struggle and doubt, they are masters at suppressing or hiding it. Stability Types are comforted by their ability to conform to social norms, either because that is their natural inclination or because it helps them to not feel like outsiders. They are determined to fit in so that they're not left out.

Stability Types are Quarterlifers whom others would describe as "solid," "normal," or "stable" in one form or other. More often than not, these are the individuals who have constructed, in the words of author Gail Sheehy, a "'false self'— a front tailored to please or to pass—that is useful in earning

approval, rewards, and recognition from the external world."
Sheehy's bestselling book *Passages*, about the stages and crises of adult development, was published in 1976, around the
same time as Kenneth Keniston's work. However, while
Keniston observed and wrote about Quarterlifers geared
toward meaning, Sheehy was exploring a very different experience in this stage of life, which she labeled the "Trying
Twenties," and later "First Adulthood."

Stability Types often present as more anxiously inclined
and guarded than Meaning Types, and on the extreme end
can have narcissistic or sociopathic defenses. Stability Types
often function by controlling their lives and others'. In particular, I've found that Quarterlifers who grew up with Meaning Type parents may hold such negative associations with
the chaos and struggle of their childhoods that they become
hypervigilant in their pursuit to gain stability in their own
lives. These Quarterlifers often try various methods to assert
control over their bodies and emotions. They may struggle
with eating disorders and have a hard time being single—the
security of a relationship, however unsatisfying, feels safer
than the uncertainty of a future alone. But at some point, all
Stability Types come to need the same thing: They need to be
able to trust *themselves* versus solely trusting established
structures or a partner. They need to trade some of the control in their lives for mystery, to let go a bit of their ability to
adapt to human society and submit instead to their own buried desires and needs. If they don't actively pursue this rebal-
ancing with other ways of being, a breakdown or reckoning
is almost inevitable—one that could destroy the stability they
worked hard to create.

Stability Types may have a level of willpower that provides them the capacity to move forward in life, but they do
not necessarily *feel alive,* or know what the purpose of their
life is. Historically, Stability Types reach their breaking point
around midlife, when the façade they were holding up begins
to crack, and they struggle to continue checking the boxes as
prescribed to them by society. It's then that they are forced to
question these external expectations and search for more
meaning in their lives. This is the origin of what we know as
the midlife crisis: a crisis of Stability Types. Those who had
successfully adhered to strict heteronormative gender roles
finally felt their inherent lopsidedness and limits later in life.
But for a variety of reasons, Stability Types have begun to
question the value of social expectations earlier and earlier in
their lives. The loss of faith that Stability Types once experienced in midlife now more frequently occurs in Quarterlife.

It's really no surprise that even the most "functional"
Quarterlifers are facing crisis earlier in life. Burnout is ram-
pant. Traumatic experiences are common. The world is in crisis after crisis. The ladders that Stability Types are used to
climbing, the boxes they are used to checking, have been increasingly rendered pointless. It's as if what they were told
was food turns out to be just clever packaging, empty of nutrition. As a result, they are left hungry, lost, and confused.

As Stability Types start to question what they've known
about their goals, their world may appear more gray-toned. It
may dawn on them that they are desperate for something
more, however indefinable and overwhelming. They begin to
seek answers to the deeper questions about who they are and
the deeper purpose of their life. At this point, they can begin

to look a bit like Meaning Types, as their personal development seeks its opposite in order to balance out. In Chapter 5, I'll dive more deeply into the experiences of Stability Types through the stories of Mira and Conner.

The Desire for Wholeness

When the social and psychological discourse on Quarterlife development emphasizes only external markers of achievement—college, job, marriage, house, children, financial safety—and not the fundamental process of *becoming oneself,* a great deal is lost. Lives are reduced to the ups and downs of successes and failures. But the search for oneself is a far more complex and extraordinary pursuit. There's a strong instinct for it. An urge to find oneself, know oneself, and manifest oneself in the world.

True adulthood is psychological. It is not about gaining stability or acting a part. It is not about procreation or a mortgage. Nor is it about adhering to personal ideologies and meaning that defy the ability to live in the world. True psychological adulthood is a kind of maturity that is about balance, a dynamic play between being part of a community and a conscious individual too. It is about finding one's way toward both stability and meaning, like a union between order and chaos, civilization and nature, or one's humanness and one's divinity. It is a symbiotic relationship in which the two parts of oneself each have a distinct role to play, like a surfboard for the ocean waves, a fireplace for fire, or a goblet for wine.

I use these various metaphors and images with clients to

help them understand their own well-being and the interplay in their lives between structure and vibrancy. There's typically an instinctive understanding for Stability Types that a "functional life" is nothing without something more, some other sense of purpose, however hard it may be to name, just as a fireplace is empty without a fire, a surfboard is nothing but inert fiberglass without the waves, and a goblet, however beautiful, serves no purpose without the wine. For Meaning Types, meanwhile, there's often an awareness of the need to develop functional structure in their lives. A fire is dangerous without the reliable containment of a fireplace; the ocean can quickly be terrifying without a platform for play; and wine can hardly be savored and enjoyed without a vessel to hold in one's hands and bring to one's lips. Stability Types know they need to work on "loosening up." Meaning Types know they need to "get it together." Often what each type knows—despite doubt and judgment—is what the other type needs for wholeness.

Beyond metaphors and personal discussion, it's impossible to easily characterize all of this in simple stereotypes. Every Quarterlifer presents differently and, depending on the situation, will feel more on one side or the other. But some examples from the public sphere can help illuminate this general polarity of types—often found in couples and sibling pairs.

Michelle Obama, for instance, called her Quarterlife self a "box checker." In this description and in the way she speaks about this time of her life, I see her as a Stability Type, one who eventually became a lawyer. However, her husband,

Barack Obama—also a lawyer—was a devoted community organizer and burgeoning author, who pondered his upbringing and what could be done to change the world. Barack Obama, I would argue, was a Meaning Type in Quarterlife who found his stability. Though both Michelle and Barack pursued the same career track, they approached life and the work differently. The well-worn phrase "opposites attract" is a common occurrence in Quarterlife relationships. Quarterlifers often instinctively seek out partners with complementary natures to help balance out, however unwittingly, their own psychology. As the Obamas have exhibited in their lives since Quarterlife, the ultimate goal for both types is to learn from the other and to stretch their comfort zones, growing toward their own individual blend of stability and meaning.

The British royal family offers a brilliant example of how this also shows up in sibling relationships through multiple generations of sibling pairs. If you've watched *The Crown* (or perhaps your knowledge of British royal history was already better than mine), you might see a Meaning Type/Stability Type split in each sibling set, resulting partially from social position and necessity, no doubt, and partially from innate characteristics. Frequently at odds with or baffled by each other, pairs of siblings can grow apart, each representing one side of the stability-meaning spectrum as it shows up in their family. King Edward, who abdicated the throne for love, was a Meaning Type, while his brother, King George, who was forced to take over as a result, was a Stability Type. Queen Elizabeth is a Stability Type driven by duty, whereas her sister, who struggled mightily to find her place in life, was a Meaning Type. Prince William is a Stability Type. He married early and has not caused much public fuss. Whatever may happen behind the scenes, he appears entirely affable and has always conveyed a sense of "having it together." Prince Harry, meanwhile, is a Meaning Type. He struggled throughout his Quarterlife as he searched for his role and worked through the pain of his childhood. He couldn't entirely maintain the royal façade in his search for a meaningful life.

In this kind of sibling pair, there's a natural balance between control and chaos. Individually, each sibling knows something about life that the other sibling needs to learn. The Meaning sibling's struggle may cause fear, worry, and pain to their family, and they may yearn for the happiness and belonging that their Stability sibling has seemingly found effortlessly within these structures. The Stability sibling, on the other hand, may likely resent the attention and distraction that their Meaning sibling's chaos inspires, but also wish for a bit of their freedom of spirit and self-expression. If each sibling can find a sense of balance within themselves by learning from the other how to manifest what they themselves lack, the impact can be significant. Psychological growth has a profound effect on the outer world. The courage to become oneself is the driving force of cultural evolution. All evolution and revolutions begin in the individual. As Quarterlifers find this balance between meaning and stability, their families, communities, and societies gain greater balance too.

The pursuit of wholeness is frequently symbolically represented in mythic stories. It may show up as the union of opposites within a single being, hero, or god. It is the half-blood wizard Harry Potter. It is Christ: both fully human and fully God. It is Buddha: alive in a timebound existence but entirely conscious of an infinite existence as well. Or it shows up at the conclusion of fairy tales as a heterosexual marriage, the coming together of the masculine and feminine, as when Cinderella finds her prince. This meeting of the opposites brings together the sun and the moon, the modern and the mythic, the human and the divine, the "rational" and the "irrational," the literal and the symbolic, the stable and the meaningful. There are countless ways that this core idea is represented, but the truth is the same: A life with only one half of the whole is lopsided. Incomplete. At some point, the urge for *something more,* however impossible to name, will beckon.

PART II

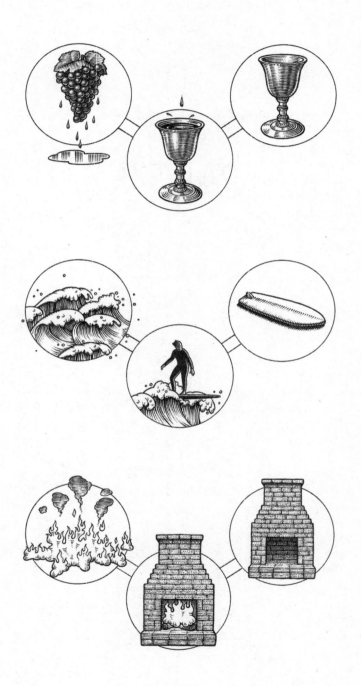

CHAPTER 4

Meaning Types

Grace

"I love your plants," Grace remarked when she first stepped into my office. She identified the plant that sat near my clock and then the little one that hung on my wall. She greeted me with wide eyes and a small laugh.

"I've been really looking forward to this." Her face was bright as we sat down across from each other.

"I'm glad to hear that." I smiled. "How come?"

"I've just had a number of friends who have benefited from therapy and I feel like it's time for me to start. Probably way past time." She rolled her eyes and sighed as if in self-mockery.

Grace had a pronounced and refined personal style: bright

pink lipstick and a jagged pixie cut of bleached hair with her natural brown color prominently displayed at the roots. She was poised and thoughtful and a little messy all at once.

I told Grace I was very glad she'd found her way here. After tending to a few logistics and paperwork, I asked her where she wanted to start.

"Well, I'm twenty-three and have yet to go to college," she began, almost apologetically. "I barely made it through three years of high school in the Midwest before dropping out to get my GED. I've been in Portland for about four years now," she continued. She told me that she'd driven across seven state lines for a girl she'd fallen in love with after meeting online.

"We've been together since," Grace remarked, making a face I couldn't quite read.

"That's a long time," I reflected.

"I feel like a burden on her a lot, though." Grace's soft demeanor cracked as she said this, her shoulders sagged forward and her eyes filled with tears. "We stress each other out. It's been hard." She started to cry and then apologized.

People hold so much emotion in, and it often shows up quickly when they finally come to therapy.

"Don't apologize," I offered. "We have plenty of time. Cry away when you need to. Blow your nose. Whatever. Your job in this room is not to take care of me or worry if you're too much, okay?"

"Thanks for saying that," Grace said, smiling through the tears. "I guess it actually helps to hear it. I do take care of people a lot." She took a deep breath, grabbed a tissue, and sat back. "I have no idea what my future is going to look like," she started again. "I think that's a lot of the problem between Stacey and me. Stacey's my girlfriend."

I nodded.

"When I'm not at work, I just spend my time trying to figure things out, and feeling crappy. Actually, most of the time that I'm at work I'm doing the same thing, if I'm honest."

"Where do you work?" I asked.

"I'm a server at a dumb restaurant. I mean, it's okay, I guess. But it feels embarrassing. I've been there for years. Stacey's a developer, a coder. She's in tech. She's paid well and she loves her job." Grace grimaced and rolled her eyes. "Ugh."

"What's the 'ugh' about?"

"Just, she's got a great job. A lot has happened for her since we started dating. Very little has happened for me . . ." Grace looked up as if to make sure I was okay before she started to cry again, and then apologized again. Then she apologized for apologizing and snorted a laugh.

Grace and Stacey sounded like a classic combination of a Meaning Type and Stability Type relationship, an unconscious attempt by both partners to find some balance through the other, and to learn what the other person knows. Stacey understood structure and the external world and modeled all of that for Grace, while Grace offered emotional vibrancy and creative inclinations that I assume Stacey admired and sometimes envied. But this unconscious trade in Quarterlife relationships can often begin to wear on the partnership as each individual evolves, or tries to.

I don't tend to do a formal "intake" in my first sessions with clients. I emphasize relationship-building over information-gathering. But I wanted to check on a few things with Grace just to make sure that she was safe. To try to gain some sense of her psychological health, I asked about how well she was eating and sleeping, and if she used any drugs.

She hummed as she thought, as if debating what she wanted to share. "I smoke blunts a lot, weed and tobacco, but not much else."

"How much is a lot?"

"Umm, I usually smoke mid-afternoon before work and then when I get back at night too. It helps me sleep."

"You have a hard time falling asleep?"

"Yeah. I haven't ever really slept well."

"Never?"

"No, not really. My mom tells me I was never a good sleeper."

"Any sense of why not?"

"Nightmares . . ." Grace scrunched up her face again. "I have nightmares all the time. Since I was little."

I could only imagine what childhood had felt like for her if she'd been having nightmares since she was a child. She seemed to be using weed so she could sleep without feeling afraid. I noted this for the future.

I looked at the tattoos covering Grace's right arm and saw that they were all plants and flowers, and on the inside of her left forearm, Gothic script that looked like it might be a Bible verse.

"What's that say?" I asked, gesturing toward her arm.

"Oh, that was the verse that got me through feeling like a freakish dyke at church in Missouri." She looked down at her arm, pointing at the words with her right hand: "*Three things will last forever—faith, hope, and love—and the greatest of these is love.*" She looked up and smiled at me, a patina of tears on her cheeks.

"That's beautiful," I told her.

"It made me feel like God would love me regardless. I would basically just stare at it in church. For hours!" She started to cackle, laughing now almost as hard as she'd been crying.

I learned quickly that Grace was comfortable with a wide range of emotions. She could go from crying to laughing within a single minute and would contemplatively reflect on her feelings.

"You got the tattoo when you were a teenager?" I asked.

"Yeah, I got it when I was sixteen. My mother had never liked tattoos, but she had a hard time really getting mad at me about it because it was a Bible verse, you know. I think she felt sort of proud underneath her anger that her daughter would rebel by getting a *Bible verse* tattooed on her arm. Like somehow she'd still raised me right."

Between being queer in a conservative community and growing up in a family that seemed to be hovering all the time just above the poverty line, Grace's childhood wasn't easy. Then there was her parents' divorce.

"My parents fought constantly," she recounted to me. "Constantly. When I was in middle school, my father left my mom and me and moved away. Then . . ." Grace looked at me to make sure she wasn't overwhelming me.

"I'm good." I smiled. "I'm tracking."

"Okay, so then, my mom moved us both to Missouri to be closer to family. That's when it got *really* bad. I had to start at a new school."

I winced a bit, concerned about what that might mean.

"Yeah. I was miserable and shy and anxious at school after that," Grace explained. "Which is why, I think, I'm so social now. It's like I'm making up for lost time!" She beamed.

Despite a long history of painful interactions with many members of her family, Grace didn't seem to express blame or feel much anger toward them. In fact, I wondered amidst all the emotions she seemed to be able to access, where her anger had gone, and if she needed any of it back.

It became clear in the first handful of sessions with Grace that she was a tremendously outgoing person. She spoke often of her large and always expanding group of friends, people with whom she enjoyed laughing and playing music, and who leaned on one another for emotional support. Her life in Portland was built around experiencing the abundance of love and play that she didn't feel growing up, and she'd done a remarkable job of finding that community for herself. Other women raised in her circumstances might have become Stability Types and chosen to bury themselves in rigorous work and responsibilities. But while Grace had helped to provide some stability to her home growing up—including getting a job when she was fifteen to help her mother with money—she ultimately felt that she wasn't "wired for responsibility and stress" as the foundation of life.

In general, Meaning Types are more oriented to their inner worlds than the expectations of the outer world. If they are oriented toward the outer world, they are likely more attuned to the suffering and injustice of others than their own personal security. As they're more connected instinctively to the wildness of life, cultural and social expectations are often irrelevant or anathema to them.

Meaning Types often have trouble with money and schedules that might strike them as "false" or "contrived." Some might even feel nocturnal, more comfortable at night when there are fewer external expectations and there's no pressure to be out in the world. This was true for Grace. She often stayed up until early in the morning, sometimes almost until Stacey was getting up to go to work. It was a source of freedom for Grace, but also a consistent feeling of shame that she wasn't as "adult" as Stacey or as "functional." Grace was happiest when her habits weren't being observed by others.

Meaning Types also often feel more connected to nonlinear time, what the Greeks called kairos, and the experience of timelessness. I had been surprised, for instance, that Grace was always on time for our appointments until I realized that she was showing up to my waiting room nearly thirty minutes early in order to avoid ever being late. Time and timeliness were a huge cause of stress in her life, but because she valued therapy, she made a particular effort to never be late. The consistency and structure of our sessions made it easier for her to trust me and feel safe. Our reliable appointments, in a reliable location, with the reliable tea in the waiting room, provided a container of stability for Grace that she could depend upon week after week. It was a schedule but with ritual, something consistent that provided ample space for her Meaning side to stretch out, structure that didn't stifle her but into which she could pour herself. This was a signal of the work we would do together.

Grace needed these structures desperately. Without them, she was prone to overextending herself for her community and then at work, until she felt that she was just a puddle of watery personhood spread across the world in every direction. Grace had a capacity to feel what the people around her were feeling. She had empathy that seemed to extend around her for miles. "I love my friends so, so, so, so, so much," Grace told me early in our work. She'd say this kind of thing often, her heart bursting with the thought of a particular person and their suffering and beauty. But then she'd get quickly overwhelmed. After too much extroverting, Grace would overcompensate with unhealthy, extreme introversion; after weeks of constant caretaking of others, she'd shut down from overstimulation and effectively disappear, ignoring her phone and becoming unreachable to anyone but Stacey for days or weeks. Grace would swing from one extreme to another because she wasn't yet attuned to what she needed, or to the importance of self-care.

The container that Grace needed is what Stacey excelled at. The structure to hold the meaning. The goblet to hold the wine. Until she built stronger boundaries, Grace wouldn't be able to metabolize all that she was trying to hold.

Meaning Types like Grace struggle to varying degrees to build up the walls they need to survive in Quarterlife. Structure is hard to develop, or it's resisted because it seems "soul-sucking." Grace needed a value proposition for developing greater personal stability that worked for her and would allow her to feel more solid on her own, without needing to lean so heavily into her relationship. She needed our goals in therapy to be about personal development, focused on round-ing her out, and not on the pejorative cultural narratives to "get real" or "grow up."

"I never wanted to be an adult," Grace explained. "Adulthood has always seemed, just like, pain, boredom, bills, stress, and meanness. It's like where souls go to die or something." Grace cackled as she said this, bending over her knees with a giggle. "Right?"

I smiled and laughed with her. "I hear you. You don't want to live the way you saw the adults around you living when you were a kid."

"Oh my god, no. I don't want that life."

Grace wanted the respect of being an adult and the freedom, but she wanted to keep her soul. After a childhood of extreme stress and alienation, Grace was trying to finally live a life that felt aligned with her values. I've never thought that such a desire was "entitled" or "unrealistic." I was happy that she still had dreams.

Supporting Grace to incorporate more stability and security in her life would be the key to building a sustainable adulthood. We'd get there through a lot of different methods, including trauma-informed therapy that acknowledged how much she had survived. It would be hard work but not just about "growing up" and "getting it together." Grace needed the goblet, but not at the cost of the wine.

Danny

"I think I'd sleep all the time if I could." Danny leaned his head against the back of the chair, his eyes closed.

"Have you eaten today?" I asked. It was 1 P.M. and I doubted that he had.

"Ummm." He paused, thinking. "I had some yogurt when I woke up? But that was around 8 A.M. I went back to sleep after that."

Danny's denim shorts were ripped at the thigh, as if they'd gotten caught on something, a flap of fabric hanging wide open. His white collared shirt was so wrinkled that I imagined it had been crumpled on the floor just an hour ago. Danny tended to be pretty disheveled, but his look also suggested a kind of bohemian lifestyle, like he lived in an artist colony on the Moroccan coast, his light brown skin tanned from lying around all day on the shores of the Mediterranean, chewing a pencil and contemplating verse. Danny was often lost in his head, thinking and thinking. He philosophized and romanticized and spent a lot of time alone. We'd been working together for several months already. In our first session, Danny had shared a number of things with me, including that he had bipolar disorder, that he was really struggling with dating for various reasons, that he had confusing physical symptoms, and that he was tired. Really tired. Danny had tried to explain to me the long saga of his exhaustion and digestive issues and the search for a solution.

"They think it might be caused by the prevalence of mold in my old apartment," he told me. "But it could also be an allergy that no one has been able to identify. Or an autoimmune disorder." He looked exhausted even talking about it all.

Some people had encouraged Danny to look into chronic

fatigue syndrome, but he also knew that a lot of other people didn't think chronic fatigue was real.

"One doctor suggested that this was all caused by a parasite I may have picked up while traveling."

But Danny also knew that the symptoms began shortly after some major life changes, so he was suspicious of the possible emotional issues involved.

"I sometimes agree with the doctors who think it's all in my head, but other times I really am so tired, and my stomach hurts so bad, that I can't imagine how that could be true. I can't make my brain tell my muscles to move me out of bed."

The collection of symptoms may have also been related to the functioning of his sympathetic and parasympathetic nervous systems, how his body was regulating digestion and rest after a single traumatic incident or long-standing developmental stress. I kept this in mind throughout our work.

It also seemed certain that, one way or another, the symptoms were tied up with Danny's overall feeling about his body.

"I hate my body," Danny told me one day, early in our work. "It's so disgusting and useless."

I didn't try to hide a cringe as I heard him speak with such vitriol. He saw me react and then defensively shrugged, while slumping down farther in his chair.

"It's just so ugly, and so not manly."

Even while questioning the gender binary and the unhealthy expectations placed upon men, Danny felt a regular, sinking feeling that he wasn't as masculine as he wanted to be.

"I honestly can't tell what's healthy for me to want, like in order to keep growing, and what are just imposed gender expectations. It seriously drives me crazy."

Nothing was cut and dry for Danny and questions of gender identity were woven into most of our conversations around identity in general. Racial identity too, as race was another area in which Danny felt himself caught somewhere in the uncertainty of the in-between. Light-skinned but with Afro-Latino blood, Danny often confounded the desire for swift racial categorization when people of all shades would ask him: *What are you?*

But when Danny felt disgust for his body it was rarely because of race, and not always a result of measuring his masculinity. It often had to do with how tired he felt, but was also related to the general experience of having a body at all. Danny hated his body because it demanded that he feed it and wash it and Danny had other "more important" philosophical and artistic things that he wanted to be doing. Danny wanted to be a writer, and I knew he had two stacks of books by his bed that he was trying to get through before the end of the year. Everything that his body required felt like an irritating interruption.

"I just wish it would do what I want it to do and then leave me alone," Danny announced one day.

I leaned toward him.

"Do you notice that you kind of treat your body like it's a servant? Like 'you're'"—I made air quotes—"the boss and it's supposed to do what you say, when you say it, no questions asked?"

Danny raised his eyebrows at me and wrinkled his nose, looking quizzical.

"But *isn't it,* kind of? A servant, I mean?"

"I don't mean to get metaphysical, but I think you need to ask yourself where you begin and end. Is your body separate from 'you' and a 'servant' of yours, or is it another aspect of you that you're sort of dragging around, miserably, on a leash while you shout at it and call it names?"

"Damn. Well, when you put it like that . . ." Danny looked back at me. "It makes me think about Belana"—his beloved cat—"and it makes me sad to think of her being treated that way."

He paused and looked out the window. I waited in silence while he thought. Then he looked back at me again.

"Doesn't everyone kind of feel this way about their body, though?'

"I think a lot of people do," I conceded. "It's part of the whole notion that we are more our thoughts than our bodies. But I can tell you, however common it is, it's not working well for anyone."

Many Quarterlifers have significant reservations about their body and their relationship to it. It may be more pronounced for people like Danny who struggle to fully identify with their biological sex and with the gendered expectations placed upon them, but sometimes the hatred of the body comes before the association to those words and ideas. Whether it's questions of gender, confusion about racial identity, fears and discomforts with sex and intimacy, chronic illness or a disability, a history of trauma, issues with food and eating, or an existential feeling of being "trapped" in a body at all, Quarterlife often involves coming to terms with being alive and embodied.

Quarterlife is a natural period of developing a conscious and loving relationship with one's body, of feeling forgiveness for its "flaws" and the ways that it has "failed" to perform or protect. It often means dis-identifying from the values of patriarchy and white supremacy that have, drop by poisonous drop, taught the majority of Quarterlifers that something is wrong with their body because of its size, shape, color, abilities, or parts. These perceived flaws can then cause countless psychological issues, all due to toxic value systems that were created by a small swath of humans throughout history and perpetuated for eons since.

I didn't expect a quick fix for Danny, and I didn't want to encourage one. This was a long-term process of facing himself and all that he'd internalized from culture and familial expectations. He had a lot to sort out between questioning his masculinity, struggling with physical symptoms, and exploring his racial identity in America. But I also thought that, like Hamlet, a Quarterlifer who famously pondered "to be, or not to be," Danny had a relatively important choice to make in facing his core ambivalence around being alive at all.

Like many Meaning Types, Danny struggled with the fundamental experience of being embodied, of being a three-dimensional flesh-and-blood person on earth, in this specific moment of time. This conundrum had to be faced as his most important first step toward gaining greater stability. Danny would need to *choose* to be alive.

"Do you think you want to be here, on earth?" I asked Danny in our first month of weekly sessions.

He shrugged in his silent, ambivalent way. Not really a yes or a no.

"I don't mean 'are you suicidal,'" I pressed. "I don't think you're suicidal. But do you think you want to do this *life* thing?"

He muffled a laugh and shook his head.

"Like if someone had given me a choice?"

"Sure, if someone had given you a choice."

"Yeah, NO!" He guffawed, almost choking. "Why bother!"

Danny kept laughing with recognition when he started to explore all this with me. His eyes widened as he chewed the sleeve of his black sweatshirt, giggling periodically and adjusting in his chair.

On the journey toward stability for Meaning Types, I think of this as the need to "incarnate." Danny would have to make a conscious *choice* to participate in existence, rather than continue to feel dragged along by time and age like a reluctant cow on a lead. It was extremely subtle, but a huge part of his growth rested on something like an invisible switch that only he could flip: He needed to *decide* to be alive and in his body. His pursuit of wholeness required that he step into life with two feet, once and for all.

"I mean, let's be honest . . ." Danny began again. "What are we all doing here? We're awful! How many police shootings happened this week? How many homeless people did I pass just to get here? How many species have we killed with climate change? Honestly, what are any of us doing here?!"

Danny was fully leaning forward now, more animated than I'd ever seen him. It was a strange but familiar juxtaposition: As Danny listed the most depressing things that we're all forced to grapple with, he was relaxed and energized. It was as if I had struck a vein and finally found his blood. He was passionate. It was a relief just to get all of these worries off his mind.

"Oh, I hear you. I struggled with this same question for years. I still wrestle with maintaining balance and hope in this world!" I offered. "But I also know that long ago, I decided to stop playing at the in-between thing. If I was going to be alive, there was no point in doing it halfway. I was going to be here completely. In *this* moment in time."

Danny looked at me quietly, thoughtfully. His cheeks were more flushed than I'd seen them before.

"You thought about this stuff?"

"For sure. Constantly." I laughed.

"Huh." He sat up straighter in his chair and took a deep breath.

"Listen, I think there's a common reluctance toward being alive in Quarterlife," I continued. "It's an ancient conundrum, the very foundation of Buddhism, right? This confusion about existence and suffering and why we're all here."

I turned around and grabbed my copy of *The Hero with a Thousand Faces* by Joseph Campbell off my bookshelf. I read a short section to Danny: "A realization of the inevitable guilt of life may so sicken the heart that, like Hamlet or like Arjuna, one may refuse to go on with it."

"Huh, yeah," Danny began. "I'm reading Pema Chödrön right now." He leaned over to his tan canvas bag and pulled out a well-worn library book by the American Buddhist nun.

"How is it?"

"Super good." He nodded as he put it back. "Super interesting. I've been reading a lot of her stuff lately."

For Meaning Types, my bid for their engagement in growing and healing often begins with a bid for their participation in life itself. Their buy-in to being alive is foundational to their progress toward stability. The encouragement to step two feet into life isn't to say, "Life is full of suffering, get over it!" but to say, "Living in ambivalence won't protect you from pain. There has always been pain in existence and being alive in these times is filled with suffering and uncertainty, but there is joy and beauty here too." The goal, I offer, is to *participate* in the world, the era, and the life that you entered at birth. Without the *choice* to live and undergo all the struggles of life, there's little that anyone else can do to flip that inner switch toward growth.

The decision to incarnate, to live life in a physical body, may be what propels many Meaning Types onto their path with the willpower and commitment they were missing. By choosing to be alive, Meaning Types have to accept being in this *specific* moment in history and this *specific* body, family, and so on. That commitment to specificity, to living *this* life, is often the hardest thing. They often think big and feel big and want to be a part of the infinite universe, or they fantasize about other times in history into which they could have been born. As a result, the decision to become embodied in the here and now can feel limiting and stifling, and filled with guaranteed pain.

"So here's my proposition," I began, looking Danny right in the eye. "I'm going to ask you, in therapy, to work on *deciding* to be alive. As strange as that may sound."

"Gah!" Danny's eyes widened in a mock fear. He was teasing, but he knew what I meant.

"I know you're tired and life feels like a drag a lot of the time. But, I think, in addition to all the other work we'll do and the philosophy and theology you're exploring, it's important to practice accepting, simply, that you're a mammal, just like Belana."

"Belana!" Danny smiled, as if remembering his cat fully in the moment. Then he scratched his head a bit and leaned back into the chair. "Okay," he said. "I hear you. I do."

CHAPTER 5

Stability Types

 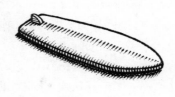 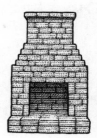

Mira

"I feel like I'm one of those stories you hear about," Mira began to tell me in our first session. "Like a person who gets in a bad car accident and survives, and then suddenly has revelations about how they should have been living their life differently."

"How so?" I asked.

"I think I need to adjust some things about my life before something really bad happens." Mira bit her cheek and looked out the window for a moment before looking back at me. "I need to figure things out. But it's all really confusing to me, honestly."

Mira was thirty-one years old and a lawyer at a reputable firm. Her clothes were often composed of grays and blacks.

She wore sweater dresses and tights, sometimes dark jeans and nice boots. She dressed carefully, but simply, as if she were always trying to disappear easily into a crowd. Mira was respectful and quiet in demeanor, but sitting with her, I got a deep sense that she was stifled and overly "in control." My own breathing often felt constricted as I tried to stay present with her tightly controlled body.

"I have this feeling," she told me after a few sessions, as she got more comfortable with me. "I have this feeling that I'm about to go crazy." She blushed as the words came out and laughed. "Oh my god. That *sounds* so crazy!"

"It doesn't sound crazy," I replied. "Tell me more."

"I just know I'm sort of lying," she told me. "It's really hard to explain."

Mira was recently married and she was happy with her husband. The previous fall, they'd had a tiny ceremony at city hall before traveling to India for a much larger, days-long Hindu wedding. She expressed loving both events, laughing as she described her husband, Tom, not being able to understand a word of what was happening during the many hours of their Indian wedding. Then Mira returned to the topic that had led us into those happy scenes. She teared up and dabbed her eyes with a tissue: she felt her husband didn't fully know her.

"I know he loves me, and he's good to me, but I keep a lot from him," she continued. "I'm not keeping secrets. I'm not doing anything bad that he doesn't know about," she was quick to follow up. "But I know that I keep a huge part of myself hidden from him. From everyone."

Mira felt out of step with herself, as if she wasn't quite living her own life. But she hadn't come to therapy because she wanted to talk about this. She started therapy because she knew, instinctively, that she had to stop hiding from herself, and others.

"I don't know what I'd even say to Tom." Mira paused, looking frustrated and defeated at the very idea of the conversation. "I'm not sure he'd totally get it even if I put the feelings in perfect terms. It's so . . ." She trailed off. "It's just so abstract."

Stability Types often feel like they're hiding, but our language doesn't quite contain the words or concepts needed to convey that experience. Stability Types, like Mira, tend to present well—as long as a true emotional crisis has not yet hit. Their lives are often quite functional, if not enviable. They have checked all the boxes and many have enjoyed doing so. Mira liked a lot of the things about her work, and she liked her colleagues. She was well paid, and her life with her husband was loving and secure. But like many Stability Types, Mira felt that something was missing. She was fine, good even, but there was also something that was terribly "off."

These ethereal feelings are often more easily captured through metaphor. I asked Mira to try to find one to help describe her inner life and she told me she often felt as if she were engaging with others through windows, or as if the world were an aquarium and she was a visitor.

"It's like this sense that I'm in the world, but no one else knows it. Like I'm watching everyone with my nose pressed to the glass."

These descriptions gave us a portal to explore together what she was experiencing, with increasing specificity and insight.

"You feel like people don't see you?" I asked.

"I mean." She paused, contemplatively. "I know people see me, obviously." She rolled her eyes a bit at herself. "But I don't think people *see* me. I don't think they have any idea that I'm often not really there."

I asked her to draw this feeling and, after some reluctance, she easily sketched a picture of a figure standing behind a tall wall, with several other figures on the other side. Then she elaborated: The wall is made of ice, and she's frozen on one side. She's there, but she's not quite involved in the world of which she's a part; she can see it all with her eyes but can't *feel* any of it.

"Have you always felt like this?"

Mira nodded. "I think so." Then she paused and looked up, searching her memory. "Well, actually, there have been a few times when I didn't feel that way."

"Will you tell me about those times? What was it like?"

"It was like laughing," she responded almost immediately, her eyes twinkling. "Or dancing without wondering who might be looking and what they might be thinking." We both laughed a little at the sudden emergence of joy from her. Her posture had visibly softened.

"Can you tell me more while you're feeling that? I want to know more about what life was like when you felt free. What were you doing?"

"I was traveling in India after college. There were a few months when I was visiting family. I started traveling in

Southern India with some cousins and friends but then . . ." She paused again, her eyes now conveying vibrancy instead of reluctance. "I stayed. I'd found a hostel that I wanted to stay at longer and I ended up surfing for weeks on the coast of Goa." Mira let out a big sigh. She shook her head as if in awe of the memories. "I'd literally wake up and surf in the mornings. I'd grab tea from the front desk and just go to the beach with whoever else was at the hostel that week. When I was done, I'd read all day. It was really amazing."

Seeing Mira light up helped me to understand who she was underneath her tightly controlled demeanor. She had clearly loved that time of her life so much, and watching her remember what it was like ushered in waves of relief. Those memories provided tremendous insight into the ethereal *something,* the sense of inner alignment for which she was searching.

Generally, Stability Types are more attuned to the external world than the internal. They're typically oriented to what they view as rational thinking, rather than the "irrational," mystical, or imaginal, and they perceive time as linear and fixed—what the Ancient Greeks referred to as chronos. In their suffering, Stability Types may feel walled off from the world. Working with them therapeutically often means trying to gently nudge them toward the opposite of their orientation: the fanciful, the irrational, the vulnerable, and maybe even flirting with irresponsibility and flakiness. They need to test the limits on how and why they live their lives, exploring what is motivating them day to day. Is it guilt or shame, or is it desire and passion? Is the life they're living the life they want to be living?

I've found that trying to do useful psychotherapy with Stability Types like Mira can also often be confounding, given how tightly they can hold themselves. They may be proactive in seeking therapy, like they know it's the next box to check. But once they walk through the door, they often want "practical" solutions. In my experience, an emphasis on cognitive work—analytic talk therapy or exercises for behavior modification—will usually stall out and feel demoralizing for the Stability Type Quarterlifer who was strongly hoping for some support in moving to the next unknown step. I sometimes feel as if I'm working against a clock, that we've got five sessions to turn their life around or they're going to calculate the cost-benefit analysis and call it quits. But the search for one's personal meaning is a long, circuitous journey, a deep exploration of what is, actually, not "practical" at all and for which there is no defined "next step."

Stability Types may feel threatened by the noncognitive, less rational work because it is so unfamiliar to them. But they desperately need some measure of the very things that scare them the most: dreams, mystery, and curiosity about the unknown. They need to remember the enormity of existence—wilderness, the night sky, the universe—of which they are not in control. Trying to help them, then, often means trying to give them a taste of their true pursuit in some visceral way. It's an effort to break out of the logical, linear, practical sphere and reintroduce them to something they may have felt, hopefully, in childhood. Sometimes, encouraging them to embrace art practices or other forms of creative exploration can help unearth these revelations. Other times, mystical and divinatory practices prove beneficial too. Mira's spark was tied into her travels, so that was my focus and where our work began. I wanted to help Mira remember the ocean, what it felt like to be traveling alone, immersed in the waves, and not always in control.

Little by little, Mira and I developed a language together around her split between stability and meaning, and how she could take that necessary step toward meaning, mystery, and wildness. Meaning is the gooey, sugary inside of a chocolate egg, when stability is the shell. It's the entire story waiting in between the secure covers of a book. Whereas stability is the feeling of safety and protection, meaning is the feeling of openness and connection. Finding this language early on helped Mira and me stay oriented when we lost our way, supporting us to come back to the memories and images that allowed her to feel the ocean, and her immersion in the world that she hoped, desperately, to experience again.

Conner

"Have you been to therapy before?" I began.

Conner shook his head while glancing between me and the ground. "Just one meeting with my family in high school, and I've seen my psychiatrist a few times for Adderall prescriptions . . ."

Conner's black beanie covered his head and a little stubble peppered his face. He looked sleepy to me. I went over a few basics from the paperwork and invited him to ask me any questions about therapy or our process at any time. He shook his head when I paused.

"I don't have any questions."

Conner had struggled to make eye contact with me when

I greeted him, and he looked nervous when I approached to shake his hand. His initial voicemail about therapy was awkward and rushed, as though he'd forced himself to speak before hanging up the phone.

"Can you tell me why you decided to reach out?"

Conner sighed and rubbed his eyes. His sweater and rain jacket were bunched up and wrinkled around his shoulders and wrists, like he'd bought them both a size too big.

"I dropped out of college," he began with a sigh. "Well, I basically failed out. My parents told me they'd kick me out of the house if I didn't start seeing a therapist." Conner looked at the ground.

His reluctance to be in therapy permeated the room. I waited for him to continue.

"I've been living back at home for months. My parents say I never leave my room, and I play a lot of video games that they think are too violent and freak them out."

I nodded, still waiting in silence. He looked at me skeptically for a moment, but I knew he had more that he wanted to get off his chest.

"I don't eat well and I don't even shower every day. I'm basically just a slob." He stared at the ground, some emotion starting to appear on his face. "I didn't used to be like this . . ." He trailed off.

"That sounds really hard," I reflected, simply. I didn't want to ask too many questions yet. "Can you tell me more?"

"I'm just so stuck," he said with a pained sigh, looking right at me. "I want to get on with my life, but I don't know how. Nothing is working."

"What do you mean that nothing is working?"

He struggled to start sentences as he eyed the aged blue carpet in my office. I had a sense that he was contemplating the path to the door and how quickly he could get out. Then he apologized for wasting my time.

"I'm sorry. I don't know." He shrugged. "I don't know. I should be happy. I should be fine. There's no reason for why I'm not happy."

Conner's pale skin tone was discernibly dulled and sickly. His blue eyes were almost clouded. His neck and shoulders appeared locked in a telltale protective hunch, and his breathing was shortened. He seemed trapped in shame like a traveler in thick fog.

As I listened and asked a few questions here and there, Conner began to share more about what seemed like a huge shift in his life recently, a shift that had terrified his family—and himself. After a while, he seemed to relax, perhaps trusting that I wasn't bored or annoyed with him, or that I wasn't going to join him in his self-criticism.

"At first, I was, like, 'on top' in college," he began. "I mean, that sounds dumb, but I was. I was on the basketball team. I was getting a ton of game time." He glanced up at me. "I did well in my classes. People knew me all over campus."

I nodded, smiling with him at his memories but anticipating the coming crisis.

"Then what happened?" I asked.

Conner looked back at the ground before continuing.

"At the start of my junior year, it all just started to fall apart."

"How so?"

"I don't really know," he told me. "That's the issue. It just all started to collapse."

Conner had done everything "right," according to social expectations. All the elements of his life had suggested relative structure and stability, but at twenty-one, everything had begun to dissolve. In the end, he'd all but failed out of college, lost his scholarships and his spot on the basketball team. As he recounted these cascading losses, I could only imagine how devastating it had been.

"I'm really sorry," I told him.

"Yeah, thanks," he responded dismissively, defending himself from my sympathy.

I knew Conner blamed himself. A year ago, the notion of failing multiple classes, losing the basketball team, and becoming a recluse had seemed the furthest conceivable future for him. He had wanted to be a top ballplayer and a straight-A student. He had been looking forward to graduating with his entire class. Somehow, he'd ended up isolated, playing video games for countless hours, barely eating, angry, and ashamed in front of everyone who knew him. After all of his work, everything seemed to disappear in an instant.

Before Conner and I had started working together, I'd received an overwhelming and anxious voicemail from his mother, in which she shared how relieved she was that Conner was starting therapy, and how worried she and her husband were. Not wanting to keep that voicemail secret from Conner, I shared with him what I remembered.

"She said that they feel like they barely know you anymore," I told him. "She said they're really scared for you."

"I think they're concerned I'm suicidal."

"Are you?"

Conner shrugged. "I don't know. Maybe."

I waited a beat, knowing this was an opening in which we needed to have a truly honest conversation about the depth of his hurt. I ventured into territory that might seem jarring to an outsider but was, therapeutically, meeting him where he actually was. If I let the moment pass without acknowledgment of what he was likely holding, all by himself, he could easily leave our first appointment feeling even more alone than when he'd arrived.

"Do you know how you'd do it?" I asked quietly, curiously. I tried to keep his eyes engaged.

He raised his eyebrows, surprised by the question. "A gun." He paused, looking right at me. "But I don't own one." He looked back to the ground. He could tell I'd ask more questions. "I don't own one, or have any plans. But that's just how I'd do it."

"But you don't want to."

"No, I don't want to. And I don't feel that a person like me should have a gun right now. But, I mean, I could get one." He started pulling at a string on his sleeve. "I just . . . I just feel . . . I feel awful all the time. I don't know how to make anything work again . . ." His face softened for the first time into what looked like grief. He stopped his breathing, to keep from crying.

I paused to give him some space before speaking.

"Can you do me a favor and just take a few long breaths through your nose?"

He did, with some effort at first, not asking me "why" or

"how," and then relaxed back into the chair with his eyes closed.

I ventured into the silence to ask what seemed like the big question.

"Do you think you ever wanted any of the things you were trying so hard to achieve?"

Conner had told me all about how hard he had worked for everything, but I'd yet to hear anything approaching joy from him, or even a genuine desire for something other than achievement or acknowledgment. More often than not, this is the kind of desire that the dominant culture encourages: Achievement over satisfaction. Acquisition over intimacy or connection. A checklist of conceptual goals that are based on social expectations more than true personal well-being. This was the script that Conner, like many of his peers, had been following since he was little. But it wasn't enough to sustain him.

"Did you ever *enjoy* what you were working so hard at in college?" I continued. "Do you remember what you enjoy?"

Conner looked back at me, as if staring through me, lost in a deep thought. Either he was remembering something from a long time ago or what I'd asked had struck a chord. He started to tear up and looked away.

I could tell in that moment that my job with Conner would be akin to coaxing a scared street dog out from hiding. I needed to gain his trust and bring him out of total isolation. But I also needed to offer things that would appeal to his instinct, like the smell of fresh food for a starving animal. I couldn't stay in dialogue with just his rational mind because his rational mind had turned rather dictatorial and sadistic. It was no longer working in his favor, a symptom of the Stability Type's pursuit of perfection and adherence to certain social values going rogue and turning rotten. Conner's operating system was focused on who he "should" be, according to social standards of success. As a result, his individual needs had been dismissed as irrational and irrelevant somewhere along the way.

Conner was a Stability Type in severe crisis. A year prior, he never would have considered therapy, and he didn't think his life choices were any cause for concern. But all the structures he'd relied upon had disappeared. I wasn't surprised that it had led him to feel suicidal. The surprising crash of everything he'd worked toward had made him feel as though life itself was gone. Conner had a single game plan, which he'd accomplished admirably: Climb. Achieve. He'd performed exactly as he'd been taught to perform. In high school, he'd gotten the right grades, and under his leadership, his basketball team had won more games than any other team in the school's history. He'd followed a similar path for his first two years of college until something dramatic changed. But the details, despite more inquiry, remained fuzzy. There was a pattern here that felt familiar to me, though.

"I think I'm getting a sense of what happened," I told him. "And I think you might be luckier than you realize." I knew I was pushing my own luck by saying so.

"You what?" Conner laughed, almost angry, his eyebrows raised in shock.

I shrugged.

"You think it's luck to feel like shit and be a disgusting blob who doesn't leave his room?"

He really hated himself.

"No," I said. "I don't. But if you'd kept on the path that you were on, I think things were bound to fall apart at some point. And I do think it's better to feel like shit and be a disgusting blob at twenty than at fifty."

"What do you mean?"

I had his attention.

"I mean that I think you're having what we used to call a midlife crisis, but in your early twenties instead."

"You think I'm having a midlife crisis?" He almost smiled, his tone starting to soften. This seemed like a much milder diagnosis than what he'd found on the Internet.

"I do. And I have a feeling that if we sort this out together— and if you start eating again and working on some more healthy routines—you'll learn some things about yourself that are really important for you to know."

Conner furrowed his thick blond eyebrows and just looked at me.

"But we have work to do. We have to focus on finding a path in life for you that feels more satisfying than the one you were on before. And not just to your ego." I paused. "I think that the course you were on before was never going to bring you the life you *actually* want."

The ladder of vertical achievements that the dominant culture raises Quarterlifers to climb leads into the ether. It's an incomplete game plan. The people who reach the top are often dangerously inflated, disconnected from the ground, and without any idea of what to do next. I told Conner that I thought he was lucky because the inflation that supported his rise had burst when he was still in college and fully able to course-correct.

While a lot had fallen apart, he still had a familiar safety net to catch him. He didn't have a career, house, and family weighing on his conscience. Conner wasn't happy being home with his parents, but he had the option to be at home. He was safe, and just starting his adult life. He had a solid chance of putting things back together again—and better.

When I offered more of this context for Conner, he was staring at me but also appeared to be elsewhere.

"Huh." He paused.

"What are you thinking about?"

"I just remembered a dream I had last year," he began.

"Oh yeah?"

"Yeah . . . actually, I think I had this dream a number of times. It always freaked me out. I was going up in an elevator at the Golden Gate Bridge . . . and the elevator stopped and I knew I had to jump through the air onto a second elevator that was passing me going up . . . I always woke up when I was taking the jump. I'm pretty sure I didn't make it . . ."

I leaned in. "That sounds terrifying."

"I was, like, *high up*. I think that's why I thought of it. In some versions of the dream, I was hanging off this bar be-tween the two elevators, like I could use it to help me get from one to the other, but I was just dangling or leaping in midair. I always woke up sweating afterward."

Conner looked back at me and shrugged, but I could see the gears were turning in his brain. He was digesting some things. What I was saying about the emptiness of that linear climb was hitting him, instinctively. Conner had felt the terror of "losing his grip" within his body. He'd struggled to stop resisting what he could sense was coming for him, whether he liked it or not.

For Stability Types, the move toward meaning frequently requires a need to "let go." This loss of control, or loss of plans, is a kind of sacrifice, the death of a former life or giving up of something that feels impossible to live without. To let go means to surrender to the end of the old way of living and to the beginning of something new. It means surrendering to one's life and path, a path that is not entirely within one's control. But this idea is hard to convey.

I've not found a simple way to explain what it means to surrender to one's path when both things are intangible—the path and the surrender are invisible. But like the feeling of falling through space or holding on to a cliff with tired fingers, the internal experiences can be described in metaphors and similes, often with the help of dreams. The need to surrender, and the corresponding fear of doing so, can be *felt*.

Conner needed to surrender control, to stop his ascent and come back down to earth where he could safely live. This sacrifice of the life he had spent so much time focusing on would require learning about the other side of life, trusting in something bigger than his willpower and plans. Amidst all of his hard work, Conner had felt like a fall was imminent and he was barely hanging on. With no training in the need for balance, and no framework for it, Conner had resisted this instinct to sacrifice some of his former plans and goals with all of his willpower. He struggled to listen to what his life or soul wanted for him. Understanding this would be the focus of so much of our work. There was so much information for Conner, and for his future well-being, woven into his thoughts, feelings, hunches, dreams, and experiences, many of which seem to have anticipated what had happened in recent months. How had Conner forgotten what he enjoyed and loved? What had truly happened at college? And what was he going to have to let go of in order to find his way back into the world?

Four Pillars

The goal, for both Stability Types like Conner and Mira and Meaning Types like Danny and Grace, is to learn the values and work of the other type. But this is not an easy sell, as each polarity is likely to see the other side in a negative light. While the other side is the antidote to their lopsidedness, it is also, usually, what they've been trying—consciously or unconsciously—to *not* be.

Stability Types might view Meaning Types as "too much." But they also secretly envy Meaning Types' connection to seemingly abundant emotion and creative expression. Meaning Types, meanwhile, might judge Stability Types as "uptight" or "privileged" while secretly envying their consistency and seeming ease in the world. All of this is culturally dependent. There are endless versions. These individuals are just a few examples of how these types manifest. But typically, within one's judgments and envy of others, one can find the projections of what they most deeply *fear and desire* for their own life. Those judgments tend to indicate the tug toward wholeness.

In reality, a pursuit of meaning for Stability Types will ultimately *support* their goals of stability, because life will feel more fulfilling, and the specter of their own felt emptiness won't haunt their sense of security. Meanwhile, the pursuit of stability for Meaning Types will support their sense of meaning because they'll be better able to manifest what they believe is possible, and they'll feel more equipped to survive and thrive in the external world.

Stability Types need to engage deeply with their self-exploration and questions of individual meaning: What brings them, specifically and uniquely, a sense of aliveness and purpose, no matter how threatening it is to the status quo? Meaning Types, meanwhile, need to wrestle with the daily tasks and long-term goals that will both help to funnel their creativity and make their lives feel more secure, no matter how laborious the tasks at first appear. Both types need to engage with healing traumas from their pasts and consciously improving the communication and relationships in their lives. The result for each individual is a nuanced and empowered person who knows themselves with increasing specificity, and is also comfortably engaged in the outer world.

The following chapters will explore this work of self-development for both types through the stories of Grace, Danny, Mira, and Conner as they work through the four pillars of growth in Quarterlife development: Separate, Listen, Build, and Integrate. These four pillars are my own adaptation and modernization of the gendered paths depicted in the stages of the Hero's Journey and conveyed through traditional rites of passage. They're also a framework for understanding the pursuit of "individuation," the development of consciousness and search for self as defined by Jungian psychology and historically viewed as work for midlife adults.

While the coming chapters are laid out chronologically, the work done in therapy is never linear in nature. It is often circular, slow, and repetitive. The four pillars of development are not, therefore, like steps on a staircase or more boxes that can be checked off a list and forgotten. As pillars, they provide points of orientation and structure, like a spider's web anchored in four places. In the weaving of a life through experience and effort, one will return to these anchors over and over again.

CHAPTER 6

Separate

*What relationships do you need to work
through, transform, or end?*

There is a natural developmental need in Quarterlife to transform relationships from earlier in one's life. It is an instinct to "Separate" from psychological and physical dependency on others in favor of new, more mature dynamics that allow for independence and individuality. However, modern life tends to drown out this instinct. From technology that makes it easier to stay in touch but harder to gain independence, to religious mandates of loyalty to one's faith and family, to low wages and a high cost of living, the profound need to separate in Quarterlife is often interrupted, resisted, and sabotaged. For the majority of Quarterlifers, the result is a great deal of confusion and suffering. Quarterlifers know they need physical and emotional space in order to sort out who they are and how to rely on themselves. But they often don't know how to separate from past relationships, or communicate their needs, let alone why they have those needs in the first place.

Countless cultural traditions of the past indicated the psychological and social need for individuals to separate from their parents. Typically, around puberty, ritual initiation ceremonies were enacted to encourage or force this shift. The customs were different depending on the culture, time, and the sex of participants, but as Joseph Campbell noted: "The so-called rites of passage . . . [were] distinguished by formal, and usually very severe, exercises of severance, whereby the mind is radically cut away from the attitudes, attachments, and life patterns of the stage being left behind." The rites attended to a natural need for the bonds of childhood to be transformed, as they are among mammals in the wild. When modern societies neglect this need for a psychological departure from one's parents and other childhood relationships, Campbell notes, an individual becomes "bound in by the walls of childhood; the father and mother stand as threshold guardians, and the timorous soul, fearful of some punishment, fails to make the passage through the door and come to birth in the world without."

Psychoanalysis has long recognized the importance of consciously separating from past dependencies and expectations, but such work has most frequently been associated with an understanding that arrives at midlife. I view that as a *mis*understanding. As I have come to see time and again, this work of Separation is a delayed need from puberty, one lost when we lost initiatory rites. It is not so much a hallmark of midlife as it is a foundational element of Quarterlife development.

Most fairy tales and myths depicting Quarterlife begin with a kind of separation in which the hero leaves home in search of something, often ethereal or strangely symbolic. Sometimes they are kicked out, banished for an inability to conform to what is expected. Sometimes they get lost and stuck out in the world, unable to get back home. Modern Quarterlifers have similar stories of initial *physical* separations. Whether it happens by force or choice, Quarterlifers can often name a burning urge to find their own way. The instinct to separate leads a person out into the world and away from their family and perhaps from their church, community, friend group, or even current intimate partner in pursuit of greater self-development or self-reliance.

Without clear cultural support to accomplish this physical separation logistically or financially, Quarterlifers are often forced to delay it. However, ignoring the instinct to separate can spark an unrelenting frustration and a sense of being trapped. There is an inner demand to start one's life, a calling for Quarterlifers to *go*, explore, and fulfill their curiosity with little regard for "logical decisions" or logistical constraints. It is a longing, a need that can't be entirely named or explained. Like hunger left unsatiated, the need to separate oneself from one's childhood home and relationships can turn ravenous when stifled. This ravenous hunger can cause anguish, panic, "drama," and anxiety. Sometimes even violence. Outsiders may see Quarterlifers in this state as "out of control" or "making things up." But for the Quarterlifer, it may feel as if they're being controlled by an alien parasite, a demanding urge pushing under the surface that they can't seem to satisfy. For some, this feeling can spark tremendous fear. They worry about the unknown, straying too far from their comfort zone, and agonize over the mortality of the people they love who have guided them. What if, like a baby forced from the womb, they separate and cannot survive on their own?

But as Quarterlifers who have already left home know, that is only the first step. To truly separate is to engage in a long process of self-metamorphosis through the slow trans-formation of financial, emotional, and psychological depen-dency in relationships. A healthy separation often involves setting new boundaries, improving the capacity for commu-nication, and sorting through all of the subtle and overt ways in which one's parents and siblings (and countless others) af-fect one's self-perception. The goal is self-knowledge, self-reliance, self-love, self-trust, and improved intimacy with others. It is often hard-won. And it often takes many years to feel that any shift has occurred.

The Courage to Claim One's Life

"They've got the right to know what I'm doing," Conner ex-pressed, obviously frustrated. It was two months into our work together and we were talking about his relationship to his parents. Any time I would begin to wade into discussing their influence over him, he'd get defensive, which, to me, was emblematic of his conflict.

When Conner had been at college two thousand miles away from home, he'd been in nearly constant communication with his parents. He didn't think he was very different from his friends in that way, and as an only child, he found some of this closeness to his parents particularly expected. His mother was the primary point of contact, but Conner knew that she was the liaison between him and his father too.

"So how often were you in touch?"

Conner shrugged. "They wanted to hear from me at the end of my games to know how they went. Even if it was just a few texts. That's normal!"

I nodded. "Totally," I agreed. "Healthy, even. What else?"

"I guess I'd text with one or both of them several times a day at school too. And they'd fly out for at least a couple of games a year," he continued. "They're super supportive people, and they're paying for college. It's not like I can just shut them out." He looked at me like the very idea was disrespectful.

"But you thought about it?"

"About shutting them out?"

I nodded.

"Well, sure." Conner looked down at the ground.

I waited. His look and the tenor of his thoughts had shifted.

"It's so stupid." He laughed suddenly, shaking his head. "Honestly, what's wrong with me?"

"Wait, what just happened?" He seemed to have been

processing something important before interrupting his thoughts with his well-worn shame.

"My parents *should* be disappointed in me. I had every possible resource a college kid could want, and I totally failed. They're right to be pissed!"

"Can we slow things down again?"

Conner took a deep breath. His conflicting belief structure was in a battle and I was trying not to allow the "rational," vindictive voice inside his head divert our session. I tend to call this inner voice the cult leader: It's cruel, controlling, and fully interested in sabotaging emotional progress it views as unproductive.

"Did some of your parents' support ever feel like pressure?"

Conner sighed and leaned back, deep into the chair. He rested an ankle over a leg and placed his palms in his lap, relaxing somewhat, like he was deciding to be in the room with me again.

"Did staying in close touch with them make it hard for you to explore your own interests?"

"I started lying to them years ago."

"Oh yeah?" I felt relief. He was back.

"I guess it's because of what you're saying, that I was lying to them because I needed space. But that sounds like an excuse." He paused. "I didn't know how to do everything they wanted from me. Or something."

"You didn't know how to do everything they wanted from you."

He nodded.

"'Cause you were also trying to do what you wanted?"

"I guess so."

"It's hard to sort through your own wants and goals if you're trying to perform for your parents' expectations all the time."

"Yeah, I guess. Yeah." He nodded and looked at his hands.

"Can you give me an example of how this might have happened? This conflict?"

Conner began, hesitantly, "I was dating a girl at school."

He stopped talking, staring deep into his hands. The energy in the room suddenly changed dramatically.

"I was dating this girl, woman, whatever. Eva."

"Eva," I echoed.

"Yeah. We were sort of together, but like, not really, for a couple of years."

"What happened?"

"I had to break it off."

"Because?"

"Because—" He stopped. His posture shifted defensively. "Because."

"Because?" I pressed.

"Because I could never bring her home to my parents. I didn't want to lead her on anymore. It just wasn't going to work."

"Wait, why? Why couldn't you bring her home to your parents?"

"It was a lot of things."

"Like?"

"Like her hair was too short."

"Her hair was too short for you to bring her home to your parents."

"Yeah. You may think that sounds stupid, but it wasn't just that."

"Keep going."

"She had a couple of tattoos . . . she was a 'free spirit,' or whatever. She never followed any rules she didn't like. My mother would have hated her."

"Did you like her?" I asked.

Conner nodded slowly but passionately for a split second and then seemed caught off guard by his honest expression of feeling. His face tightened, as if a sobbing sadness was about to rush out of his throat. He looked away and reached for his water and took a drink. Then he stared at the glass, lost in thought.

I sat in silence with him for a bit before gently continuing. "How did it end?"

Conner shrugged and looked away again. "I just started avoiding her."

"You started avoiding her," I quietly reflected.

"Yeah."

"Did she know why?"

"She probably figured it out."

"You never told her."

"No, I never told her. I just ghosted her. I couldn't deal with it." The volume of his voice dropped a bit. "Honestly, that's part of the reason I hide, I think." He paused again, his water in his hand. "I miss her basically all the time."

Tears threatened to overflow. He brought the glass up to his lips again but didn't drink at first. He looked back at me.

"Is that fucked up?"

Conner was meeting my gaze now, the glass on his thigh.

I knew he hoped I'd say no to his question. He wanted abso-
lution for his behavior, and for the guilt that I now realized
he'd been carrying. But absolving him of his behavior wasn't
my right, nor something I could honestly do. He needed to
face the relational ruptures that were causing him pain, and
learn from them. He needed to acknowledge the deep grief
and loneliness he'd been feeling since cutting out his friend
and companion, someone whom he had clearly loved a great
deal. When a person can honestly confront and process grief
and guilt, the opportunities for growth in intimacy are huge.
I tried to bring us back to the core of what was happening.

"So, to this day, you think that Eva has no idea that you
disappeared because of your parents, and not because of
her?"

"No. I mean, I blocked her on social media and everything. I said some pretty mean shit to her too . . . I just tried
to hate her so I could get her out of my mind."

I sat with him in silence.

"But it wasn't just because of my parents," he continued,
defensive again.

I imagined he'd had this debate with himself a thousand
times already.

I have found the devotion to parental expectations among
the trickiest things to sort through in Quarterlife because the
devotion itself can be so unquestioned. Respecting our parents is socially and intellectually defensible as "good" and
"moral." In many cultures and communities, it's rule number
one. But Quarterlifers' instincts demand evolution away from
their roots, sometimes with tiny whispers and doubts, and
sometimes with shouting demands. There's a natural neces-

sity to separate from parental dependence and influence. But because we are so accustomed to listening to our parents, and because there's so little social framework for shifting away from their beliefs, parental perceptions often carry more weight than our personal instincts. Carried on too long, that childhood fealty can become psychologically dangerous. You can't serve two conflicting masters simultaneously without losing your mind.

Until we started digging into this together, the discord between Conner's future and his past, his parents' desires for him and his own desires, wasn't conscious. It was just frustrating. Deeply frustrating. So Conner had defaulted to doing what he'd always done: trust his parents, or try to. And now he was in a dangerous bind. Conner had wanted to be in a relationship. He'd loved being around Eva. He'd loved that she was "a free spirit," and I imagined that he'd thrived on her energy when he allowed himself to follow his own curiosity and desire. She sounded like a Meaning Type who could awaken his own sense of freedom, instinct, and joy. But Conner had ultimately shoved all of those feelings away in an unconscious choice to remain loyal to his parents, perhaps his mother in particular, who represented a very different way of being and didn't seem to hold back on her anxiety about his future. Until Conner could face the risk of disappointing his mother, Separating from her anxiety, and endure whatever judgment she may have of him, he'd continue to feel stuck in his life, unable to choose the relationship—or anything—that was genuinely good for him. He'd drive himself and every future partner crazy with mixed messages and an inability to commit. And his resentment, even hatred, of his mother would also grow. This, unfortunately, is an extremely common pattern among cis male Quarterlifers today.

Conner wasn't comfortable acknowledging that he had grown instinctively beyond the reach of his parents. He wasn't yet decisive or courageous enough to step into the life he wanted, and as a result, he was trapped in limbo, a purgatory, where he neither went after his own life, nor lived up to his parents' expectations. It was the worst of all worlds. After a while, he couldn't identify how to make any decisions at all anymore. Completely paralyzed, he had just crashed.

I tried to explain all this to Conner.

"Does it make sense?"

He nodded, leaning back comfortably in his chair.

"Yeah, it actually makes a lot of sense," he began. "I do feel like I'm in purgatory, but I haven't really known why. I thought I was being punished for something."

Conner was going to have to develop the courage to take responsibility for his own life, his own desires and choices, regardless of how far away from his parents' desires they led. This courage didn't necessitate disrespect to his parents, however. That depended partially on how they chose to respond. His work to separate could involve a great deal of communication and attempts to share what was happening for him, and what he needed. But it did necessitate the fundamental acknowledgment that he wasn't on this earth to be their clone, nor their protégé. He existed in order to be *himself* and to sort through, carefully, what that meant. Learning about who he was and living that self would be his magnum opus.

I hoped that Conner's parents would follow his lead. Author Audre Lorde wrote enduring guidance from a parent's perspective for how to support healthy Quarterlife development. She expressed that every family member must feel free and empowered to live their own life. Writing specifically about the experience of mothering a young man, Lorde emphasized the value of *her own* psychological health and vibrant life as a model for his development: "The strongest lesson I can teach my son is the same lesson I teach my daughter: how to be who he wishes to be for himself. *And the best way I can do this is to be who I am* and hope that he will learn from this not how to be me, which is not possible, but *how to be himself.* And this means how to move to that voice within himself, rather than to those raucous, persuasive, or threatening voices from outside, pressuring him to be what the world wants him to be." (Emphasis mine.)

Parents who struggle to let go or trust in their child's capacity to find their own path can help the entire family system by turning their attention toward themselves. Parents can only parent adults if they have done their own work to separate from their own childhood relationships and pursue the lives they most want to live. Just as their children need to go find their new, independent lives, parents need to do the same. More than during any previous developmental stage, parents of Quarterlifers can't base their sense of identity on the experience of parenthood. They often need to face beginning again, and pursue living *their own distinct identities* if they've put things aside in order to focus on parenting. Parents need to explore their own ambitions, creativity, fears, and hopes, and courageously move through their own psychological obstacles.

The hope is for parents and their Quarterlife children to

be able to evolve toward being equals on the road of life, with less hierarchy and dependency than ever before. But this transformation of roles requires a great deal of conscious work because parent-child relationships are riddled with pot-holes of pressure, misunderstanding, hurts, failures, and, un-fortunately, abuse. To those ends, the parents of Quarterlifers can often benefit from therapy as well.

Conner wasn't in charge of his parents' emotional or psy-chological growth, and from where I sat, it was a bit hard to know who was overwhelming whom. Everything was mixed up with stress and anxiety. But I was pretty sure that before Conner could develop the courage to fully honor his feelings for a girlfriend, he would need to find it in himself to defend his *own life*. In many respects, this work is the beginning of the development of moral courage in general. To separate in Quarterlife is to build awareness of the influences and pres-sures from other people on one's own perceptions and choices. And so, the work to separate is both a psychological necessity and an ethical one. Separating "what I believe" from what others believe in a nuanced way builds an informed con-science, and enhances the capacity to trust the course of one's own life, even—or especially—when one's own standpoint conflicts with the status quo. This is the ability to know who one *is* and *is not,* and to know where one stands in conflict when there is ambiguity or pressure to conform. Without this self-knowledge and allowance to defend *his own needs,* Con-ner would never be able to truly honor someone else's desires and needs in a relationship, and any creative life he'd ever hope to have would suffer under the constant fear of judg-ment.

Conner and I spoke about this aspect of his development over months. We strategized talking with his parents and then processed together how those conversations went. What began with him leaving notes for them on the kitchen table became hours-long discussions, sometimes all together and sometimes with just one parent or the other. I was grateful to hear, after a while, about his parents' receptivity and their collective family progress. None of it was easy, but it seemed clear that the overall weight in the household began to lift. There was more mutual understanding than there had been before.

Getting to Self-Reliance

"I don't want to use her," Grace related to me one day. "And I know I am. I'm even manipulative in ways that make me cringe. She's too good to me."

Grace was reflecting on her relationship with her girl-friend, Stacey, a topic we'd been exploring on and off for months. Grace wanted to tease out why they were still to-gether, and if it was healthy for either of them.

"It just makes me feel like a lazy child. I don't want to feel that way anymore."

Grace was beginning to sound more resolute than she had in past sessions as she tried to understand this vague inner pressure to be on her own, an urge to be alone that didn't conform to practical notions about her overall stability but was unrelenting nonetheless.

"I can't stay with Stacey because I'm scared I won't sur-vive without her." She looked straight at me with clarity.

"I hear you," I said. "You don't want to be reliant on her."

"Yeah. I can't rely on her. I don't want to have to rely on her."

Grace's initial process of separation had begun early in her life when she began questioning the Church and her mother's strongly defended beliefs. It continued when she met Stacey online and left home, physically distancing herself from her mother and making a decisive move in the direction of her own life. But now, after four years with Stacey, Grace's work to clarify her own identity seemed to be unfolding on another level, as she started to shift out of her first committed romantic relationship.

Heterosexual marriage was once the social standard for how to separate from one's parents in Quarterlife, the dominant path in which a Quarterlifer left their childhood home and began to create an independent life and family. For many, as was true for me, marriage has been replaced by college as the first move away from home. For others, joining the military or getting a job in another state is their way out. This form of separating, however it unfolds, has historically been an unrefined and unconscious process.

Early Quarterlife marriages have historically served social and economic needs more than psychological ones. For this reason, midlife crises have often been correlated with divorce, as well as a reevaluation of unprocessed parental relationships. But individuals like Grace highlight the myriad ways that separation can occur in Quarterlife. She left home for a relationship, but not marriage and children. Her questions about what she needed in life didn't have to be put off for a decade or two.

Grace, neither married nor straight, was in her early twenties and was already engaged in a process of carefully discerning in what ways she was relying on her partner but not necessarily fulfilled by their relationship. The relationship with Stacey had helped her to separate from a home life and belief system that did not feel right for her, but the limits to growth within her partnership had started to show too. However irrational or unnecessary it seemed, Grace felt she needed something else.

"I have this sense that if I don't end the relationship . . ." Grace paused mid-thought and clutched her stomach. "Ugh. This is seriously so nauseating to think about. I don't know if I can do this . . ."

We both waited in silence as she processed what she was feeling.

"I know . . . I know that if I don't get up the courage to end things with Stacey, we'll both just be stuck. I don't want that for either of us."

"Say more. How will you get stuck?"

"I mean . . ." She took a deep breath. "Stacey, like, reminds me to eat. She makes sure I'm opening my bills and paying them on time. She helps me fall asleep at night . . ." Grace gasped almost silently in that moment and began to sob. She bent over her knees, a sudden wailing grief pouring out of her.

I leaned forward instinctively too. "That's the part that scares you the most, huh?"

Grace kept crying, just slightly bobbing her head to me in agreement.

Grace knew that her girlfriend helped to balance her out and that it was grounding, stabilizing to have her around. But for most of the time I'd known her, Grace had explored with me the ways she also felt that her girlfriend was unintentionally coddling her. Sometimes Grace wondered if Stacey was almost trying to keep her attached. It was all very confusing; she couldn't entirely tell what was true, but Grace knew that as much as she loved her girlfriend, she was ultimately using her more as a crutch than a joy. More than anything, she was sick of feeling like a burden, or like a little girl who couldn't survive on her own. Grace had shifted her reliance on her mother to Stacey; she had never truly been alone. So in therapy, and outside of therapy in her journal and with a couple close friends, Grace began sorting through what she needed and wanted, little by little.

Grace was working on understanding what was hers and not hers, who she was and was not. This work of careful discernment can also prove necessary for Quarterlifers with siblings, whose individual identities are often built on these complex bonds, as well as those with close friends, whose pacts to remain close can inadvertently stifle individual expression and growth. Similarly, Quarterlifers can feel an inner, quiet drive to separate from their religious group, as Grace did, or from their political affiliations, if their evolving self no longer conforms to their earlier allegiances. The work to separate involves a lot of what the pioneer of family systems theory, Murray Bowen, called "differentiation," or "the differentiation of self." The idea is critical to Quarterlife development, differentiating the "me" from the "not me."

People who are poorly differentiated from others, Bowen noted, are more prone to overwhelm. Meaning Types, like

Grace, can often struggle to differentiate because they tend to value community and connection and may actively reject notions of individualism in various forms. But the inability to differentiate *my* feeling or opinion from *their* feelings or opinions can create stress akin to a computer short-circuiting: There's just too much information and not enough clarity on how to process it all. There's no individual sense of self in the sea of others.

Grace's love of her community and her empathy put her at high risk for this kind of continuous overwhelm. It was almost impossible for her to say no to anyone, but she needed to set boundaries and claim alone time. She needed to do this to be able to separate her thoughts, needs, and feelings from those of others in her life, and to work to build greater stability on her own, rather than depend on others to provide it for her.

About a year into our work together, after a lot of careful conversations, I opened the door to my waiting room to see Grace sobbing as quietly as she could, mascara running down her face. She melted into the chair in my office.

"We broke up last night," she sputtered in grief. "I'm so sad!"

Grace cried for at least twenty minutes as she recounted what had happened, telling me all the things she and Stacey had talked about. But after a while, when the tears stopped and her boisterous laugh had returned, she hadn't changed her mind.

"I know it's the right thing to do. I want to be on my own for once."

Making Peace with the Past

"I wanted to run away. I couldn't look him in the eye. But I, like, also really wanted to be as close to him as I could, you know?"

Danny had never told anyone this story before, the story of visiting his father in the hospital after he'd crashed his truck while driving drunk. Danny had known that his father drank too much. Alcohol had always been an issue in his household growing up. But he'd never seen his father like that before: injured, fragile, and scared.

"I just remember the awful look on his face. He was so withdrawn and depressed-looking." Danny took a deep breath and looked up at the corner of the room. "Seeing him there kind of broke us . . . or broke me."

Danny rubbed his forehead and started crying. Silent tears ran down his cheeks.

"God, it was awful."

We'd arrived here, at this story he'd never shared before, because it was also the story of how Danny had been diagnosed with bipolar disorder in his freshman year of college. Only a few days after seeing his dad in the hospital, Danny returned to his campus, several hours away by car. He knew that there wasn't any way for him to be helpful at home, but Danny began to struggle in his classes.

"It was like I just couldn't stop worrying. Maybe that's what happened? Or maybe I'm making excuses." Danny paused, still thinking out loud as he worked through what had unfolded those first months away from home. He leaned over his knees a bit and rubbed his scalp, the hair on his head just stubble. "My grades were terrible that semester. Like I seriously think I failed two classes!" Danny laughed, self-mocking and ashamed.

When he was back home for summer that year, Danny stayed with his mother, stepfather, and several of his siblings. He remembers his mother remarking over and over how different he seemed.

"She spent most of the break, like, checking on me. '¿Qué pasó, mijo? What happened to you?'"

"She was really worried," I reflected.

"She was." Danny nodded. "I think she was so worried at the time that I'd end up like my father."

Danny's mom scheduled an appointment for him with a psychiatrist. She encouraged him to give the doctor a full family history, including his father's alcoholism, and the fact that his dad had recently been diagnosed with bipolar disorder in the hospital. It was a diagnosis that she'd found clarity in after her own years of struggling with Danny's dad.

"When you went to that first appointment, do you remember what the psychiatrist asked you about?"

"Honestly, I don't really," Danny began, leaning back. "It was years ago. But I don't think he asked me very much. It wasn't a very long appointment."

"Did you tell him how you'd been feeling after your dad's accident? About how worried you'd been?"

"I think so? Maybe not. But he seemed focused on my dad's alcoholism and the fact that my dad is bipolar. I think maybe he and my mom had talked too?"

"What happened afterward?"

"I mean, that was kind of it. I left with a diagnosis and a prescription."

"How did that feel at the time?"

"I don't know," Danny replied, looking back at me. "I guess I felt sort of both relieved and—" He paused and sighed, like preparing to confront something big. "It was honestly three things, I think, all mixed together."

Danny stuck out his index finger and began to tick things off a mental list.

"I was relieved that I had an explanation for why I'd been feeling so terrible." He held up another finger. "I was freaked out that I was like my father, in the worst ways. And three," Danny held up his ring finger, "I think . . . this is crazy . . . after feeling so worried about him after the accident, I was sort of comforted to be connected to him again. Even through a diagnosis."

Danny was nineteen at the time, and it would have been a huge thing for him to understand all on his own. I appreciated how carefully he could discern what he'd felt back then, trying to piece together what had unfolded.

The psychological work required to separate one's own identity from the identities of parents (and siblings, friends, partners, and so on) comes in every conceivable form. For Grace, the struggle with differentiating from her mother hadn't been terribly difficult because she could clearly see where her mother's values diverged starkly from her own. But Grace had to work harder to clarify who she was with her community of friends and with her partner. Conner had years of acute work in front of him to learn how to be radically honest with himself about the life he wanted, and to pursue it, no matter the opposition from his parents. For Danny, the work was different again. It wasn't that Danny's father was exerting subtle or overt pressures. Nor was Danny feeling that confused about his overall values in relation to his parents. In fact, Danny felt more or less politically aligned with his mother, stepfather, and father, and somewhat remarkably did not feel much conflict with any of their belief systems. But, like many other Quarterlifers, Danny's struggle lay primarily in the subtle, almost sacrosanct questions of self and identity. In this case: his bipolar diagnosis, which he'd been told he inherited from his father and that he would have, unchanging, for the rest of his life.

After Danny recounted the origin of his diagnosis, we spent the rest of that session clarifying what his symptoms had been at the time and since. I wanted to explore whether such a diagnosis felt accurate to him.

"Do you remember the psychiatrist telling you much about the diagnosis at the time?" I asked Danny, leaning in, my elbows on my thighs.

"The doctor explained that I'd inherited my dad's bad genes and that I'd need to be really careful to take my medication."

"Did *anyone* ever ask you about the grief or worry you were feeling after your dad's accident? Or about how you were adjusting to being away at college for the first time?"

"No." Danny paused. "I don't think so?"

I scrunched up my face and looked down at my feet. Then I looked at him, catching myself. I was trying to stay impartial, but failing.

"I'm sorry for the faces I'm making." I was the one thinking out loud now. "I feel sad that you weren't given more space to sort out everything that was happening at that time in your life. I'm frustrated that you probably could have used someone to talk to, or to answer your questions about what was happening with your dad. And I'm frustrated that instead of getting someone to talk to, at least to start with, you were given a diagnosis and pills."

"Yeah." Danny looked into his hands in his lap and then up at me. "That probably would have been helpful."

I paused to let my own protective inclinations toward Danny, and Quarterlifers in general who have received quick-draw diagnoses, calm down. This wasn't just about Danny's diagnosis for me and he didn't need to carry my own frustrations.

Mental illness, like personality traits and physical vulnerabilities, can certainly be inherited. But that inheritance is not a foregone conclusion, and not every moment of pain that a Quarterlifer experiences will be a harbinger of the same issues that their parents faced. Unfortunately, the diagnosis of mental health disorders tends to be a painfully imperfect, subjective endeavor. For Quarterlifers, life changes tend to be *constant,* and experiences are often overwhelming. The result can be all sorts of emotional ups and downs that *may* be expressions of mental illness, and *may* benefit from medications. But they also may be indicative of a person sorting out existence and dealing with life events.

Danny looked up at me and we made eye contact. I exhaled deeply and smiled.

"You don't think I'm bipolar?" Danny named my hesitations directly, curious.

"Listen," I began, a bit haltingly. "I think it's worth exploring again whether you need to be on this medication or not. According to what you've told me about that time when you received the diagnosis, you were: grief-stricken, scared, lonely, maybe traumatized by seeing your father in the hospital, and depressed, certainly. But other than your father's own diagnosis, I'm not hearing any reason why *you* would be diagnosed with bipolar disorder."

"Huh." Danny paused. "Yeah . . . Huh."

"I don't want to rush into a judgment, but back around the time you were diagnosed, there was a significant uptick in the number of kids and college kids being diagnosed with bipolar disorder to try to explain what was happening for them. And to be clear, some folks *should* be on medication who aren't. There are many, many people who benefit from their diagnosis and medication. Based on what you've told me, and how you're feeling, I'm just not sure you're one of them."

I wasn't sure how Danny was taking this and leaned back in my seat to give him more space before continuing with one final thought.

"Look, the truth is that *I* feel sad when I see people starting their independent lives with something that can feel like a lifelong curse, a diagnosis that is supposedly inherited and will never change."

Danny cocked his head, looking at me as though through only his left eye, like a bird curiously assessing a passerby.

"It does feel like a curse," Danny said. He straightened his head again and looked right at me. "But, I mean, isn't it, kind of? I mean, my dad is an alcoholic and bipolar."

"Well, this is where *your work* is needed. When it comes to alcohol and substances, you probably need to be careful for sure. We all benefit from knowing our family histories and family vulnerabilities. But you're also a totally different person from your father. And as for genes, the field of epigenetics now clearly confirms that our genes aren't as fixed as we once believed. The environments we're in and the ways we treat ourselves have a huge effect on how the genes that we inherit express themselves in our own lives."

"Huh." Danny looked thoughtful and tired.

"I think there are reasons to doubt the certainty of the diagnosis you received, and the need for you to continue taking your medication. At the very least, if you're up for it, I think it's worth having a full intake and discussion with another prescriber. I want you to have a chance, at *this* point in your life, to sort through what happened back then and who you are now." I paused. "Do you have interest in exploring this, or should we leave it here?"

"No." Danny looked right back at me. "I do want to explore it."

As a psychotherapist, I don't handle medications and do my best to refer clients, when necessary, to a prescriber with whom they can have full conversations about symptoms and goals. My preference is to work with medication prescribers who also take nutrition, lifestyle, trauma history, and community support into account, versus focusing solely on family history or the current expression of symptoms. Unfortunately, more often than not, due to a combination of spotty insurance coverage and long waits for psychiatric appointments, this can prove extremely difficult. But that day, with Danny, we got lucky. I gave him the name of a nurse practitioner with whom I'd worked in the past and whom I trusted. They were able to meet for an initial appointment within a few weeks, and Danny was able to ask all of his questions and offer a full background. The two of them agreed, in that session, that Danny could slowly go off of his bipolar medication. She gave him clear directions on how to cut his dosage. The three of us would then monitor changes in symptoms closely to see how Danny was feeling week by week. Meanwhile, Danny also left her office with some suggestions for a morning and evening dietary routine that might support his digestion. It was practical, proactive, and useful information, and Danny was relieved.

"She had a cat in her office too!" Danny beamed. "A big ol' tabby cat."

I smiled in response, so grateful to have a colleague available to offer accessible, humane clinical support, and for Danny to be able to rely on another person's knowledge as he sorted out, bit by bit, what he *had* inherited from his father and what he had not. With the right kind of support, Quarterlifers can grow far beyond their parents' wounds. The widespread notion that such a thing is impossible, or that mental illnesses are fixed conditions, never changing or transforming, can interrupt necessary self-reflection and stall the motivation needed in Quarterlife for healing and growth.

In addition to this meeting with a prescriber and our weekly sessions, Danny needed to engage directly with his father. What he felt he'd inherited from his dad went far beyond just diagnoses. Danny knew that a lot of his ingrained perception of how to be a man in the world was developed from his lifelong observations of his dad. He'd watched his dad drink and make crude jokes with friends, trying to pull Danny into gatherings that had always made him feel uncomfortable. But mainly, he felt determined not to have the relationships with women that he'd watched his dad have over years—beginning with the stress Danny felt his father had caused his mother. We talked a lot, Danny and me, about toxic masculinity and what *healthy* masculinity could look like for him. I suggested that part of his work might also involve attempting a correspondence with his dad. Danny wanted answers to some things that had happened in his childhood and with his parents' divorce, and he wanted to name some of the harmful ways that masculinity had been modeled for him. In truth, he felt he needed some apologies in order to move forward.

This attempt at a dialogue with his dad was courageous emotional work meant to consciously separate his sense of self from his father. And yet, the goal was not to get further away from his dad and double down on "being nothing like him." It was, in fact, to try to get *closer*. It was an effort to *understand* his father—and thereby himself—in new and profound ways.

Danny began by writing a long letter to his dad, asking questions he'd never asked and expressing things he'd never expressed. Danny didn't know if his father would ever write back. But one afternoon, Danny arrived to therapy with a letter he'd received in reply, a shockingly present and contemplative response from his father: a man who, it turned out, had been in therapy himself for years. Danny hadn't known that, and there was so much more that he began to learn about his dad's life. Eventually the two of them started talking on the phone, conversations that weren't always easy, and that sometimes required Danny to acknowledge his own mistakes and misunderstandings too. The conversations afforded them both ways to deepen their relationship, and to offer apologies and forgiveness. They were working to separate their lives so they could *both* live more fully in the here and now, and be connected with one another through a conscious *relationship* instead of through shared pasts, trauma, or diagnoses.

Going It Alone

"We'd had a really nice visit a few months before she died." Mira's voice was steady but strained. "It was just after she'd received the diagnosis. I flew straight back home and started accompanying my parents to my mom's doctor appointments."

"So it was a really sudden diagnosis?" I asked.

Mira nodded.

I was still learning the details of how her mother had passed away about five years before.

"Yes, very. She was fifty-four when she died. It happened so—" Mira looked away. "It happened so, so fast."

Mira looked absentmindedly out the windows at the buildings and sky. Memories were starting to come back to her viscerally.

"I was the first one to really understand that she was

going to die, I think. The doctor said something about treatment options, but I know what 'stage four' means. They can
give you options, but once it's in the liver like that . . ." She
trailed off.

Mira looked down and her face began to flush with emotion. She grabbed a tissue and just held it, crumpled in her
hand, thinking.

"She never had a thought for herself," she continued,
looking down into her lap. "I think we all realized that she'd
been having digestive issues for months, and that she didn't
talk about it. She never told us. She just adjusted her diet in
ways that she thought would help."

I was getting a sense of her mother's extreme fortitude and
self-sufficiency, for better or worse.

"Honestly, I'm not sure it would have made a difference if
she'd told us," Mira continued. "The cancer was probably
too far gone anyway, but it does make me angry to even consider it, thinking about what could have happened if she had
sought help, or if my father had insisted that she see a doctor."

In her early thirties, Mira was, I realized, partially in therapy and starting to "do her work" psychologically because
the loss of her mother had changed everything for her. Grief
often forces a kind of life review. It's an experience that no
one wants, but it's also an emotion that tends to put everything into perspective. Unlike Conner, Mira's life as a Stability Type hadn't collapsed; she'd been able to maintain
momentum, but the impact of that loss had been lingering in
the background for the past five years.

"You never sought support for grief after your mother
passed away?" I asked Mira.

She shook her head.

"I think I was just in 'go mode' for so long, handling the logistics of my mother's memorial, and then supporting my father through his grief and all the help he needed now that my mother was gone. My brother too. He started to spin out. I had to try to keep him on track."

"It must have been a lot."

"It was crazy. I think those first two years were a blur. I was still working most of that time too. There were times when the grief was so bad that I'd have to call in sick," Mira shared. "But for the most part, I'd just cry in the shower after work."

Mira grabbed her tea from the side table where it had been cooling and took a sip.

"Can you tell me more about your mother?"

She swallowed and nodded.

"She lived for me and my brother. Not, like, in a pathetic way. I think she was actually really happy being a stay-at-home mom. She loved cooking, and she loved playing cards. She'd play cards with my aunties Thursday night at the house. They'd each bring a dish to share. Some Indian dish. My mother was always in charge of the naan and the chai. She loved those nights! They'd play cards late into the night. My dad would go to bed without her!"

Mira laughed at the memory and I smiled with her. But it was clear that in that memory, happy as it was, she was deeply lost in thought.

The work to separate looks very different when parents have passed away or are unavailable for interpersonal work. Conner had to learn to communicate with his parents and set boundaries. Danny went into deep repair work and relationship-building with his father. Grace had countless conversations with her partner. But while Mira was able to talk with her father, she was no longer able to process the past with or ask questions of her mother. There were things she wished she'd said, and milestones she wished her mother could see.

I've had clients do this separation work with parents who are gone for all kinds of reasons: they are in jail, they died by suicide or were murdered, they abandoned their family, or they're so abusive that the process of separating requires strong boundary-setting more than any kind of dialogue. When a parent has passed away, is unavailable, or was never present to begin with, separating in Quarterlife means doing the methodical work of identity development through memories, stories, or physical objects that are left behind. Sometimes it means family research and asking others about their memories, or reading old letters and journals to search for answers to burning questions or unformed hunches about one's history. It's a difficult process when feelings of anger, grief, pain, and joy arise and there's no one with whom to wrestle, to ask questions, or to ask for forgiveness. There's no one around to say "it's okay" when you want to change directions in life. No one to go to for blessings. No one to say "I'm sorry" when an apology is deeply needed. Mira had to sort out this part on her own. Most burning, she needed to give herself permission to begin untying her mother's desires for her life from her own.

"She wanted something else for me." Mira had a clear, straightforward look on her face.

"What do you mean?"

"Being a housewife and stay-at-home mom, she told me a few times, when it was just me and her, that she wanted me to have a career. That she hadn't had that opportunity as a young bride in India. She wanted that for me, a full intellectual life."

"Was she specific about the kind of career she wanted for you?"

"No, not really. In a way, the family line was still that I should 'find a nice Indian boy to marry,'" Mira said, shifting into an Indian accent for emphasis. "But I knew that it was kind of for show for everyone else. My parents were more progressive. My mom, in particular, didn't truly want that for me."

"So she was glad when you went to law school?"

"She was thrilled. She sobbed at my law school graduation, and celebrated every good grade and award. She was amazing."

Mira started to cry more outwardly now, drawing the tissue in her hand up to her eyes as her breathing began to sputter.

"But what if I don't want to be a lawyer anymore?"

Mira had placed her central concern now squarely on the table.

"You don't want to be a lawyer anymore?"

Mira shook her head, then said under her breath, "I don't think so."

"Did you ever want to be a lawyer?"

Mira shook her head again. "I don't think so."

CHAPTER 7

Listen

Can you hear what you feel, want, and need?

The second pillar of growth in Quarterlife is to "Listen." In addition to the courage and capacity Quarterlifers develop to separate from relationships and perceptions that no longer serve them, Quarterlifers need to turn a focus on learning to listen to themselves and begin to take seriously what they hear. Learning to listen to oneself means hearing and understanding all sorts of nonverbal information like hunches, feelings, physical sensations, synchronicities, silence, and dreams. The dominant culture rewards material success and a certain level of conformity. But psychological maturity necessitates the development of one's innate individuality. Perhaps ironically, individuality is honed through a *relationship* with one's self, an attuned ability to listen to one's own wants and needs. Though some may be quick to shallowly interpret this as narcissism, the goal is nothing of the sort. A true witnessing of oneself involves radical honesty, a lot of humbling, and a commitment to hear internal guidance even when it moves against the status quo.

Each of us has a body from which to learn. We have a spinal cord tapped in to a central nervous system that mediates our inner relationship with the external world. There is sensory awareness that is constantly being filtered, providing us with a continuous subtle awareness of our surroundings. The act of listening to ourselves is aided by learning to read these cues from our bodies, demystifying the experience of intuition. The more enhanced this connection to one's own sensory perception and inner world, the more one's unique life path can be uncovered and walked.

But the practice of listening can help on a day-to-day basis with well-being and orientation too. We all experience "ups and downs" and may get so far away from our bodies that we can feel dangerously "high," as if with an inner experience of vertigo; other times, we feel leaden and "low," like we can't quite stand up. Sometimes, we feel "spun-out" or "disoriented." Sometimes we are prone to feeling "flooded" with emotion, or we fear we might "lose control," struggling to "keep it together." When we're feeling better, we feel "grounded" or "in balance" or "centered." We can take note of how a comment or a look from someone "knocked us down," or "boosted us up." We can learn to notice, when we feel these things, what may have precipitated the change and what we might do differently next time.

Sometimes it takes patience and time alone to really think back, or feel back, to when the sense of "instability" began. In noticing those things, the availability of information unfolds: What can be attended to in the future for both greater stability and greater fulfillment? What boundaries can be set? What playful experiences can be engaged in with oneself or with others? What foods or sleep habits can be adjusted? The more we can develop this awareness of our own inner states, learning what may have triggered a dangerous emotional collapse or an inflation, the more we can attend to psychological well-being as a *practice*, something to exercise and improve at, not simply something to fall victim to and about which to depend upon others for answers.

In fairy tales, the ability to listen is often what distinguishes a hero from every other character. When the cursed dogs bark, the hero can hear their specific cries for help when no one else can, and learns how to free them, thereby earning the treasure that the dogs had been protecting for centuries. When the birds arrive to help the hero with an impossible task, the hero is receptive to their aid; she does not shoo them away in fear or irritation. These moments test the hero's capacity for receptivity over mere effort, willpower, or bravery. Does the hero listen to the talking animals, or mock them? Does the hero accept the help of scurrying ants, or stomp them? These stories explore a hero's ability to defer to hidden wisdom, often found in irrational or illogical places.

Listening to oneself is all about gaining orientation and recovering one's instincts. It is Luke Skywalker training and practicing to use the Force. Once Luke could connect to this mysterious ever-present *other*, he'd learned how to trust something beyond what he knew in his mind. The partnership of those two ways of knowing—a sort of intuition combined with rational knowledge—is what gives the Jedi their strength and wisdom. These mythic stories provide guidance on how to walk into an independent life, a life in which one no longer makes decisions solely in deference to an authority, but through discernment, self-knowledge, and self-respect. It's work that can be derided as "weak" and "sensitive," but that actually takes tremendous skill.

The knowledge gained by listening frequently moves contrary to the dictates of the dominant culture, drawing more on a form of knowing that is often associated with indigenous and genderqueer people. For most people, proper listening involves a humbling of the ego and often an acceptance of what is considered "woo woo" or "witchy" to patriarchal white supremacy. Indeed, learning to listen may even involve leaning into divination practices like astrology, the Tarot, or the *I Ching*, or similar spiritual or religious rituals. It may mean developing a greater relationship to land, animals, and plants. Learning to Listen will likely be supported by journaling, dreamwork, active imagination, meditation, or simply time alone. It often requires paring back on external noise: socializing less, disengaging from technology, sleeping more, and healing from trauma and addictions that cloud consciousness and alter the ability to hear or express one's needs. Whatever one's method, I think of this practice as putting up antennae to gather information on one's life that wouldn't have been easily heard before.

But listening also requires *discernment,* not just blind faith. Discernment is defined as "the ability to judge well" or "the ability to show good judgment about the quality of something." It is the capacity to use oneself as a reliable filter. Whole groups or movements espousing counter-culture beliefs and practices are frequently just as detrimental to the genuine work of learning to listen to oneself as the dominant culture.

Ultimately, the practice of Listening simplifies decision making in one's life. Quarterlifers are often paralyzed in the face of decisions because they don't know who or what to listen to. Fundamental to psychological maturity—and to a healthy society made up of those people—is the ability to think for oneself, to be able to tell right from wrong regardless of the perceived "rightness" or "wrongness" of those around you. Ultimately, after a lot of trial and error, the goal is to be able to listen to cues within oneself without strain or worry, just as the Jedi feels the Force.

Healing the Trauma

"You think that has something to do with why I can't sleep?"

It was months after Grace had moved into her own studio apartment. She was feeling good about the decision, in many ways relieved to have alone time. But she still wasn't sleeping well, and being alone at night felt overwhelming. We'd been getting deeper into her trauma history, exploring how the lingering effects of two decades of stress could be the cause of her insomnia.

"I think, for various reasons, your childhood was pretty

scary and hard," I reflected, responding to her question about sleep. "I think your body isn't sure when it's safe to relax, or doesn't fully know how to anymore."

Grace seemed to ponder what I'd said, but looked doubtful. "But aren't there a lot of people in that kind of situation? Scared as kids, I mean?"

I nodded. "Too many."

"Then what's my problem?"

"Well, just 'cause a thousand kids are suffering doesn't change each individual child's loneliness and pain, right?"

Grace nodded and shifted in her seat. "We live in a seriously messed-up world."

Her eyes were cocked in wry frustration as she slipped off her shoes and pulled her stockinged feet onto the chair.

"I guess." Grace paused, trying to gather her thoughts. "It's just, I mean, I get what you're saying, but it wasn't that bad!"

"Your childhood?"

"Yeah! It wasn't, like, an actual war zone or something."

"Right."

"I mean, hasn't everyone survived stuff?"

Most therapists are familiar with this kind of uncertain protest from clients when exploring their trauma history. The majority of people, it seems, struggle to acknowledge their pain when they compare themselves to others. It's part of the defense system that protects us when we get hurt, the "it could have been worse" defense. Meanwhile, other Quarterlifers don't want to face the extent of their trauma history because they think doing so will make them look or feel weak.

"Have you heard of the ACE Questionnaire? 'ACE' stands for Adverse Childhood Experiences."

Grace shook her head. "No. I haven't heard of it."

"It's a short series of questions that can help to define, simply, how much stress you were under while you were growing up."

Grace raised her eyebrows.

"Would you want to take it with me now?"

"Sure," she responded, her left shoulder shrugging up toward her ear.

I pulled up the ten questions and began moving through them with her, reading each one aloud.

"Before your eighteenth birthday, did a parent or other adult in the household often or very often swear at you, insult you, put you down, or humiliate you? Or act in a way that made you afraid that you might be physically hurt?"

"Wait, repeat the first part?" Grace's feet were under her now, she was sitting up straight, alert and curious.

"Before your eighteenth birthday, did a parent or other adult in the household often or very often swear at you, insult you, put you down, or humiliate you?"

"Ha!" Grace laughed out loud. "Oh yeah . . ." She drew out the last word like she was about to start singing. "Yes. All the time." She started laughing again. "Oh, this is easy!"

As we kept moving through each question, Grace's demeanor softened into contemplation.

"Was a household member depressed or mentally ill, or did a household member attempt suicide?"

"Yes."

"Did you often or very often feel that your family didn't

look out for each other, feel close to each other, or support each other?"

"Yes. I guess. Yes, that's true."

She responded yes to several more. By the end, Grace's ACE score was 7 out of 10. The higher the score, the more "adverse" the childhood.

The ACE Questionnaire is a simple, no-nonsense quantitative indicator that helped Grace see for herself, without qualifiers or defensive explanations, how painful things had been for her growing up. When she wanted to reassert "It wasn't that bad!" we could slowly break down what "that bad" must mean—sometimes teasingly, sometimes seriously— if her ACE score was 7 and if she wouldn't wish any of the things she'd lived through on another person or animal. Though she wasn't readily able to acknowledge it, Grace's childhood had been filled with chaos and uncertainty, and Grace had layers of attachment trauma to work through.

Grace had been caught in a state of traumatic response since early childhood. She'd struggled in school and felt stuck with career prospects not because of inherent character traits, but because of the years of accumulated grief and terror that she'd always kept to herself. She was incredibly resilient and had learned how to survive and thrive in her own way without tending to healing her trauma. But often the resilience that carries a person through childhood can start to wane in Quarterlife, when our natural defenses start to wear down and all sorts of previously buried symptoms begin to emerge. For many Quarterlifers with chronic stress and trauma histories, the early years of this stage are like the first minutes of swimming in a powerful current. It might feel difficult, but also energizing. However, as time passes, the exhaustion inevitably sets in. In their "freeze state," many Quarterlifers maintain a heroic form of resilience, until the fatigue mounts amidst the seemingly unrelenting river of life. The resilience starts to disintegrate, revealing layers of despair and panic underneath. Pretty soon, they can be swept downstream. If a trauma history—large or small—is present, the process of healing from trauma needs to be a core component of learning to listen to oneself. The voices of past trauma and toxic patterns will compete with the trustworthy voices of one's own animal body and needs. Hard work is needed to demystify and untangle this information internally because Quarterlife need not feel like a constant swim upstream.

Meaning Types, like Grace, can also be overwhelmed by sensory and intuitive information, so the practice of listening also involves learning to distinguish *what* to listen to. Some people use drugs or alcohol to help blunt the sensory overload, just as Grace turned to cannabis to help her fall asleep. Often, she was so overstimulated that she struggled to maintain focus. Week after week, she'd collapse like a puppet at the end of a show. If she was going to be able to listen to herself and what she needed, she'd need more silence and more space.

"I remember the panic attacks starting early on," Grace shared. "But I didn't know what they were called back then."

Grace stuck out her tongue in disgust and squirmed in her seat. She pulled her knees up close to her chest, her long white tube socks facing me.

"I can't even—" She paused. "I can't even believe, honestly, that I survived them. They were so awful, the panic attacks, and they happened so often. My mother called them 'Grace's drama.' She'd slam her bedroom door on me and keep me locked out on the other side."

"How old were you?" I asked her.

"I think they started maybe after my dad left, after we moved, but they got really bad while I was in high school. Before I dropped out. Maybe fourteen? Fifteen?"

"What happened in high school?"

"Well . . ."

Grace shared with me that in high school, when she was just barely a teenager, she had been subjected to relentless public shaming for supposed promiscuity.

In high school, when sexuality is brand-new and when the strict definition of gender roles begins to control social dynamics, this gendered, biased, and abusive hazing of young women and queer youth is extremely common. I've heard similar stories from clients regularly, as well as from young men who recount the exhaustion of trying to keep up with old-school bravado, and who feel ashamed of their behavior, or were shamed and hazed themselves.

The shaming that Grace experienced had been severe. The harassment at school drove her to one suicide attempt before she dropped out as an act of self-preservation.

"I think the rumors about me were started by a guy I'd kissed on a date but didn't want to see again. I didn't really like him, you know? But I was still trying to figure out if I liked guys at all."

Though she sensed she might be attracted to women, Grace tried to date boys for a while to deflect attention. She was so ashamed of being gay, so overwhelmed by the harassment by her peers, and so isolated in her relationships that despite everything, she didn't try to seek help. She hadn't felt there was anyone to protect her. Before and after dropping out of high school, the panic attacks seemed to have taken over her life.

"I'd lie down on the floor against my mom's bedroom door, like right against the crack of the door, to get as close to my mother as I could. Even though she didn't want to deal with me. It was the only way I knew to try to soothe myself, I guess. I just didn't want to be alone."

Grace's body was now in a tight ball, her arms wrapped around her knees.

"I hated myself for how crazy I'd get, but I never knew what to do about it. I could never stop myself from crying. I just felt like I was dying all the time."

"I'm so sorry," I said quietly.

"I feel like my skin is buzzing." Grace's voice was low as she looked at me, bringing us back into the present moment.

I knew what she meant by the buzzing.

"Let's stand up," I suggested.

Grace put her feet down on the ground and squirmed again in the chair, arching her shoulders and back like a cat preparing to fight. I stood up and she followed.

"I'm going to ask you to punch that pillow." I eyed the big pillow that Grace has just been leaning against.

"Punch it?"

"Yeah. I wish we had a punching bag in here, honestly, but we work with what we have."

Grace looked back at me, doubtful.

"Don't think too much about it, okay? Just go. If you feel

safe doing it, just punch that pillow like you're really mad at it and don't stop until I tell you to stop."

"Okay," Grace remarked, confused. She took a deep breath and started casually punching the pillow.

"Faster," I instructed. "Like you're pissed."

We'd worked together for over a year. Grace trusted me, even when I was suggesting strange things, like now. She punched faster.

"Harder!" I directed.

Grace began punching the pillow harder and harder. Soon, her intellectual reluctance gave way and she was fully there, her body and fists moving rapidly, strength and energy manifest in the room. Then, suddenly, she was sobbing.

Grace's punching slowed as the tears began.

"Keep going if you can," I encouraged, softly. "Try to keep punching through the tears." The back and forth movement, in addition to the physical release, is incredibly valuable for emotional processing, especially if it can be maintained for a bit through grief.

Grace kept punching the pillow until she was wailing in tears on the ground and I kneeled down with her. I placed my hand on her back as she cried and cried.

"Let it out," I encouraged gently. "No need to hold anything back."

A few minutes later, Grace was wiping her tears and blowing her nose with a bundle of tissues. We were back in our chairs and looking at each other in silence.

"What was that?" Grace asked me, surprised by the feelings that had emerged, as if from nowhere.

"That was a form of trauma release," I offered. "Your

neck and shoulders have been holding on to so much 'fight' energy for so many years. I imagine you wanted to kick the shit out of all those people in high school to protect yourself, but couldn't. So instead, it's just been trapped there, stuck in your body."

Grace chortled a laugh as she blew her nose again.

"That energy of self-defense gets stuck in the muscles when it can't be used. There's a lot of wonderful research going into learning how to release those traumatic experiences from the body so you don't have to carry them around anymore."

"Wow. Yeah. I'm"—she looked up at me, depleted—"I'm exhausted. Like deeply exhausted."

"Yeah, I bet. Can you just go home and take a nap now?" I asked.

She nodded.

"Go home and drink a lot of water and sleep," I encouraged. "Try to stay away from substances and your phone for the rest of the day. This was a big release and you need to give yourself space to metabolize everything."

"Yeah." Grace nodded. "Damn. That felt good, though."

"Yeah, I bet." I smiled seeing the relief on her face.

The techniques for trauma healing that I use with clients are varied and adapted from the work of a number of healers, like EMDR (Eye Movement Desensitization and Reprocessing) from Francine Shapiro; Somatic Experiencing from Peter Levine; and other leaders in the field like Bessel van der Kolk, Resmaa Menakem, Judith Lewis Herman, Stephen Porges, and Gabor Maté.

Sometimes, Grace and I would just work with foam balls

or a sweatshirt in her hands. When she was sitting down, I'd encourage her to squeeze her fists in a bilateral movement, activating her shoulders and arms to release tension the way a cat does while kneading a blanket before curling up to sleep. Increasingly, Grace found her own rhythm with this during our sessions, sometimes moving quickly, sometimes slowly, sometimes standing up to punch the pillow again. It didn't always provide a big release, but it usually calmed her. To support the "flight" energy trapped in Grace's legs, I also taught Grace the yoga posture "horse pose," which resembles riding a horse, with a straight back and bent knees. I wanted Grace to have some things she could do anytime on her own to help ground herself when she was overthinking or felt anxious. Horse pose helps to draw anxiety that is caught in the chest and shoulders down into the core, thighs, and feet, where it can be more effectively processed and released. I encouraged Grace to allow her body to *shake* anytime that buzzing energy of grief, anxiety, or stifled rage pulsed through her. A leading expert in body-oriented therapy for the healing of psychological trauma, Peter Levine discovered *shaking* or trembling as a natural form of trauma release, particularly in mammals and birds. Humans tend to suppress the natural inclination to shake due to embarrassment, confusion, or fear. But it's a simple, instinctive process that the body utilizes to prevent becoming stuck in a state of fight, flight, or freeze.

Grace was proactive with her self-care and, given all that she had to heal from, I was very glad for that. I wanted to help her learn to pay attention to her body and to the unconscious memories—including those of resilience—that had gotten buried in her muscles and skin. Our goal was to move the memories that had overwhelmed her and had been left unprocessed to a place where she could metabolize them, just like any other memory or experience is "digested" through sleep and dreaming. Rather than experience these memories as toxic invaders to fight, her body could instead begin to view them as food, incorporating their nutrients and expelling the waste. In the end, the memories could make her stronger. This was psychological alchemy: transforming the chaos of her childhood into her creative and emotional gold. It wasn't work to be romanticized. But it was powerful when it unfolded. "While trauma is hell on earth," Levine wrote, "its resolution may be a gift from the gods." To my mind, the goal of all trauma-informed therapy, and psychotherapy in general, should be one of full escape from hurt and an *embodied experience* of freedom, autonomy, and *joy* in the physical world. For many Meaning Types like Grace, this is part of the journey to trust that the world is now safe enough to hold them.

Over time, Grace began to sleep better. She began to emphasize self-care in a new way. In particular, she began practicing listening for when she needed alone time versus time with friends, a difficult thing for a person who once cared so deeply about having people around her and felt scared to be by herself.

"I'm also walking for at least an hour a day lately," Grace shared with me, catching me up on some changes she'd been making recently to her weekly routine. "It's such a relief. I bring my phone for music, but I turn off all the other notifications so I don't get interrupted." She was practicing being alone without feeling lonely.

"That sounds amazing," I reflected. "And calming."

"It is. It's so calming. I don't even necessarily walk the whole time, sometimes I just look at the flowers in people's yards or start chatting with a dog walking by." She giggled. "Sometimes I just lie in the park at the church by my place and stare at the trees."

The image of her on the grass, taking her time, made me happy.

"I love that." I smiled.

Hearing the Other Side

"It's so funny. For years I've been so glad that I'm not like my brother, and now I'm afraid I'm going to turn into him." Mira was biting her inner lip and staring out the window. It was pouring outside.

"Tell me more. I don't know much about your brother yet."

"He's really smart, but he can barely keep a job. My dad has been really worried about him. I mean, I am too, but . . ." Mira's face took on a look of exasperation. "I've just wanted him to get his shit together."

"And now?"

She was contemplating something deeply.

"Now I just 'get him' more than I used to . . ." Mira continued to stare at the rain, seemingly thinking it all through.

It became clear that Mira and her brother had the classic two-sibling split: one Stability Type and one Meaning Type. It's common for siblings to play off of each other as they develop, judging each other and admiring each other for a lifetime. One builds brick walls for protection, a sturdy fireplace to protect against fire, while the other is driven to experience the warmth of the flames, regardless of risk. The former can seem cold but more put together, the latter can seem passionate but like they don't have a clue. Though the presentation will certainly look different depending on the people, this same polarity exists in families of all types, from low-income to middle-class, to the sibling pairs of the British monarchy, as I explored earlier.

It's not unusual for Stability Types to look down on or fret over their Meaning Type siblings. The Meaning Type may struggle to hold a job or keep a partner, only enhancing the Stability Type's worry, while also cementing their own determination not to be similarly "dysfunctional," "embarrassing," or "crazy." The result is that Stability Types, like Mira, may just keep building up walls to contain the chaos, only to realize they've actually built a wall around themselves instead: They're lonely, bored, and lack the sense of the clarity they expected after working so hard. It's at that point that they may begin to see the value in their Meaning Type sibling's orientation. They may start to envy their sibling's capacity to take risks and live seemingly without worry about what other people think of them. Mira, in thinking about her brother, began to wonder if maybe there was some meaning to his madness.

"I get now that he's going after something that was missing for both of us in childhood," Mira continued. "I've been trying to do what our parents wanted for us and looking down on him for not doing that. It wasn't conscious. But I realized that I think he's been trying to figure out who he is. What he likes."

I listened intently as Mira worked through this idea.

"I think maybe I've always resented his freedom? Like it scared me to live with so little structure. He believes in things. He has conviction. He's not always right, of course." Mira rolled her eyes.

I smiled and laughed.

"But he cares about stuff and follows his heart."

As she spoke, I saw that Mira's brother might provide us with a road map to understand her own evasive longing, little by little. Speaking about her brother allowed us both to imagine the kind of "chaos" or mystery that would help to balance out her order.

Mira was still consistently working seventy-hour weeks and didn't seem to have any other passions or interests. She'd been driving herself hard since practically kindergarten, always the one in class who raised her hand first. She was "put together" and "on top of everything." But now her foundation was starting to crack.

She'd been in therapy with me for around eight months. In general, she was feeling less isolated from her husband, Tom, less off in her own world that he barely understood or even knew existed. It had taken a number of conversations with him to explain what she was learning in therapy, but they were talking more about things that she'd never shared with him. She'd expressed feeling seen by him in a way that she'd not felt before. As Mira continued to separate herself from her mother's hopes for her, she had to continue exploring what *she* wanted. She now knew that she'd never wanted to be a lawyer. But what she *did* want was still far from clear.

In each session, we listened together for specifics about what Mira wanted for her life, gaining information bit by bit. We needed tangible people, images, and ideas as Mira practiced how to hear her soul-self. It was a side of her that, in a way, she'd let her brother carry all these years. She needed to let that part speak clearly, without shoving the voice away into work or empty distractions.

After learning more about her brother, I decided to start exactly where we were.

"I'm really curious about that other path that you might have taken, this side of you that you now see your brother living, in a way. Can we explore that together?"

Mira nodded. "Sure."

"Okay." I turned around and grabbed some paper and pens from the small, old hutch beside me. "Can you draw something?"

Mira nodded again and reached for the pens and clipboard that I had in my hands.

"Just draw a couple of stick figures to start. One on each side of the paper."

"Just stick figures?"

"Yes, just to keep things simple for now," I responded. "I'm going to ask you a bunch of questions and we'll fill things out."

Mira picked a teal pen and drew two stick figures, one on the right and one on the left.

"Okay, good. Now take some time to feel into those two sides of yourself that we've spoken about in the past," I told her. "Try to really tap into this. From what I understand, there's the side of you people know: the lawyer and wife. And there's this other side that I'm still learning more about, the single woman who loved traveling, for instance, and loved surfing, and who maybe feels a bit more like her brother."

Mira looked at the paper as if the ideas were already filling up her mind. I almost felt like I was interrupting when I added instructions.

"Just choose one side for each of those people, those two sides of you, and start writing descriptions about who each one is."

Mira bit the inside of her cheek as she stared at the page and began writing, head down.

"Just words?" She looked up at me again. "Descriptors?"

"Words, yes. Anything you feel like. Anything that comes up. Consider them as two actual people inside of you, as much as you can. Think about how they might dress. What jobs they have. What their love life is like. What part of the world they might live in. Just explore them as people—real, distinct people. See what shows up."

Mira began writing before I was finished and over many minutes, she wrote what came to her and went back and forth between the two sides. The paper was filled with teal words, the pen in her hand occasionally drumming her thigh as she thought.

"Okay." Mira put her pen down and looked up.

"Great. Let's start with you sharing what you noticed," I prompted her.

"Well," she began, "they're very different. This one is a corporate lawyer, right? She is analytical and smart. She's paying all her bills, you know? She's safe. She's married. She has a house. She likes to go to the farmers' market—which, I mean, *I* don't actually ever go, but I feel like she does."

"Awesome. And what about the other one?"

"This one is much looser. She's more, like, boho. She has a loft in a city somewhere, and she eats lunch in the sunshine, in the middle of the day. She sort of struggles to pay her rent but it doesn't seem to worry her that much? She has lots of friends and she paints every day. She wears overalls without a shirt on and just paints . . ."

I raised my eyebrows. "She sounds pretty cool," I commented.

"Yeah . . ." Mira trailed off as she took in her own thoughts. "I used to want to be a painter."

"You *did*?" I had never heard Mira even mention art before.

She nodded.

"What happened?"

"It just didn't seem practical to do that, you know? Like who actually paints for a living?"

"Do you ever paint anymore?"

Mira shook her head. "I did all through high school, but I stopped after a couple of classes in college. It just didn't make sense to keep working at it." She paused.

I waited.

"One of my professors in college told me that I should consider really pursuing it. After that, I never signed up for another class again."

"Because it scared you?"

"Yeah, I guess. It was like, if I kept going, I'd get locked in.

I'd love it too much or something. I knew I couldn't want that future." Mira looked down at her hands. Her long, straight black hair fell over her shoulders.

"But you miss it," I reflected.

Mira's eyes filled up with tears. "Yeah." She was surprised at the feelings. "I guess I do really miss it, huh?" She brushed her hair out of her face as she sat back against the chair.

I was relieved to see Mira's face flush with emotion. As she teared up and released these memories, she felt present in the room with me in a way she rarely had before. Here was the fire, the spark I'd seen when she spoke about traveling, the heat she needed to melt the ice wall that kept her from the world and from a deeper relationship with herself. We were finding where her Meaning side resided, and what brought her a sense of embodiment and purpose. Mira was listening.

"Do you think you can give these two women names?" I asked, looking at her paper.

She gave it some thought and wrote two names down, one on each side.

"The lawyer one is 'Jennifer.' I don't really know why. It's just the name that feels like her." She suddenly laughed out loud with a thought. "I think she's like my whiter self, like my more American, grew-up-in-the-suburbs side."

"Like more of what you've learned to be in order to fit in?"

Mira nodded in strong agreement. "Totally. She's trying hard to fit in."

"And the painter? What's her name?"

"The painter is Mirabai." Her face flushed as she said this, and then she choked up as she started to speak again. "Wow.

This is so bizarre! I can't believe how emotional I'm getting!" She took a deep breath. "Anyway. Mirabai. That's what my family calls me."

"Mirabai," I reflected.

Mira now looked different and felt different, and even in her emotional state seemed much more relaxed. I was pulled toward her by the life she was now exhibiting. It was pulsing through her and in the room. We were experiencing each other's presence more than we had before, and with more ease.

"So." I paused, looking right at her. "Do you see that your work right now is to help Mirabai thrive?"

Mira nodded.

"Do you see that until Mirabai is thriving, you won't be thriving?"

Mira nodded again and wiped tears away with the heel of her hand.

I sat then with Mira in the loaded, energized silence. Something potent was happening, and connections were being made.

I've found that this simple exercise has tremendous potential to help people experience their inner civil war, the struggle between their Stability side and their Meaning side. When finding internal information with which to listen to oneself is difficult, as it can be for tightly wound Stability Types, exercises like these can be incredibly helpful. Similarly, typology tests and personality indicators from Myers–Briggs to the Enneagram to personal astrology and beyond can help Quarterlifers explore themselves from multiple angles. The goal with any of these exercises, as always, is to hear the information that is generated with a fully discerning ear, sorting through what is true and untrue about oneself versus swallowing whole any imposed perception.

I glanced at my clock.

"Can we do one more thing before we end for today?" I asked Mira, wanting to make sure we captured the essence of things.

She looked at me and nodded. "Yup."

"Draw a couple of circles. We're going to make two simple pie charts. Above one, write 'Current,' and above the other, write 'Ideal.'"

Mira did as I asked, grabbing a magenta pen for this part.

"Now, without overthinking it, just draw two pie charts for the balance between these two people inside of you. What's their *current* balance, or share of the space inside you? And what's your sense of what would be *ideal*? In other words, what's the balance that would make you feel whole, or aligned within yourself?"

Mira again took to this pretty instinctively. The clipboard was on her lap tilted up toward her. I couldn't see what she wrote, but she told me when she finished.

"Current is 90 percent Jennifer and 10 percent Mirabai." She paused. "And Ideal is 10 percent Jennifer and 90 percent Mirabai." She cringed.

I raised my eyebrows. "Wow. So, you can imagine, I guess, why you're not so happy with things right now . . ."

"Yeah." She laughed. "It's pretty bad."

"You want to be 90 percent Mirabai."

She nodded. "It should be the opposite from what it is. Jennifer can be super helpful, but she needs to be supporting Mirabai. Instead, she's burying Mirabai with tasks and jobs and errands because . . ." She tapped the pen on her leg. "Honestly, Jennifer is terrified of how different Mirabai is. But they're both miserable. Mirabai is miserable and lonely. Jennifer needs to learn to chill out."

We both laughed out loud. She was seeing herself with compassion and humor versus stress and shame.

I'm always impressed by how deeply a person can identify their two sides and the relationship between them. I loved hearing Mira express so clearly how these two huge parts of herself were interacting, and what they needed.

I told Mira how much more connected I felt to her now that Mirabai was here too.

"I feel it too." She took a deep breath.

We sat in silence together as Mira stared at her paper, lost in thought.

"I have to talk to Tom again," she declared, softly.

"What are you thinking?"

"I think I need to admit to myself and to him that I'm really not happy with my career and that . . . that honestly it's just become an addiction."

I took in her own self-witnessing for a minute before speaking.

"How do you think that conversation will go?"

"We'll see. He's very comfortable with us having two good incomes. He wants to buy a house this year. But, he's also very supportive. He knows I'm not happy."

"He knows you're not happy."

"Yeah. I'm not happy." Mira looked contemplative.

"Because Mirabai wants to paint," I reflected, bringing us back to where we began.

"Yeah, she really does." Mira nodded thoughtfully, staring out the window again at the rain.

Learning What You Like

"Do I have any control over any of this?" Conner asked me one afternoon, a sort of terror in his voice.

"Control over what exactly?"

"Like all of it. Why did this all happen?"

He was anxious but stifled, suppressing his feelings and gripping his hands tightly, rubbing them at times like they were in pain. He had weeks when he seemed to be making progress, while others felt like a deep slump. Now he was ruminating aloud again, wondering what had become of his life.

I looked at Conner in his gray sweatshirt, the name of his college in green capital letters arching across his chest. I flashed back to the dreams that he'd shared with me, dreams in which he'd been perpetually rising in an elevator, going up and up, waking as he was leaping from one elevator to another one, attempting to go higher still. The question of choice was a tricky one.

"Do you remember those dreams?" I asked him. "Do you remember the feeling that woke you up? You were so high off the ground, jumping or hanging in midair."

He nodded, curious.

"I think something was happening inside of you for a long time, long before you dropped out of school," I began. "I'm not sure you have control over it so much as an opportunity to participate with reality." I paused. "Your reality. Do you know what I mean?"

"Not really, no." Conner shook his head, a skeptical look on his face.

I didn't want to get abstract and lose Conner. I tried to collect my thoughts.

"I think you were climbing too high in your life, seeking accolades and your parents' approval. Maybe the Adderall was involved too?"

Conner just glanced up at me briefly, not saying "yes" or "no," before looking away. I'd gauged that there wasn't space yet to talk with him about whether he might be abusing the drug.

"Whatever it was," I continued. "Something major was off. You weren't living in your body, connected to gravity. Your unconscious was reflecting that clearly. I don't think you were connected to your *actual* life, you know? I think your dreams knew that it was only a matter of time before you were going to crash back down to earth."

"You don't think I was living my real life?"

"Do you?"

Conner paused and shook his head again. "No. It's strange. I don't get it. But I know what you mean."

"Can we start today with some breathing?" I wanted to support him to shift out of his head and into relationship with his body.

He looked up at me, uncertain.

"Your breathing is short and I think it's contributing to your anxiety and stress. The air isn't reaching your whole body or brain. It's stopping about here." I gestured to a couple of inches below my throat. "You feel that?"

Conner nodded, contemplative, as if noticing that stuck sensation in his upper chest for the first time.

"Let's start here. There's no way for us to really get you feeling better without lengthening your breathing, okay?"

"Okay." Conner was tentative, but I pushed ahead, knowing that the little bit of breath work we had done together already had helped considerably to quiet his mind.

"Start by bringing your awareness to your body. See if you can notice the edges of your body and how it meets the chair, and the ground, and the air around you." I paused.

Conner nodded, and I waited a bit.

"Now see if you can feel the air as it touches the insides of your nostrils," I continued. "Notice that gentle sensation, the movement of air as you breathe in . . . and out."

Conner closed his eyes without my prompting, bringing his awareness to those sensations and away from what had been happening, involuntarily, inside his chest and throat.

"Now, without forcing anything, try to lengthen your inhales and exhales," I said in a quiet drawl, attempting to slow things down. "A slow inhale . . . and a slow exhale . . ."

Conner had been so agitated that very little changed at first. I felt like I could see the speed at which his mind was running. But he didn't protest my suggestions and we kept breathing together. Then I asked Conner to add one more piece: a swallow at the end of his exhales.

"Take your time and see what it feels like. There's no perfect way to do this. Just notice if you're able, after you exhale, to pause . . . and then to just . . . swallow."

I watched Conner struggle with this at first, an unexpected

and strange movement. Sometimes, when people's breathing is sped up or shortened, the encouragement to pause and swallow can evoke a feeling of choking, a primal fear that they're not going to get enough air. I nudged Conner to move through the resistance that might arise around the act of pausing his breath.

"Listen to your own body," I said again quietly. "Always listen to your own body. If any of this is ever too overwhelming, listen to yourself instead of me. It might feel scary at first."

He nodded softly.

This additional movement of swallowing can slow the mind down dramatically. It can help to reset breathing and teach the body that it is safe, that it does not need to panic.

After a very short while, Conner began to appear more comfortable. His cream-colored skin appeared more robust, flushed, healthier, and then he suddenly inhaled as if after a long cry, catching his breath in two relieving waves.

After another minute or so, I invited Conner to open his eyes again, and he did so gently.

"How was that experience for you?"

Conner smiled as if drunk, a little delirious but happy. His eyes were markedly brighter.

"I feel good . . ." He paused. I smiled just looking back at him. "I don't think I've ever actually breathed before in my life. I feel good . . ."

The entire room felt quieter then, as if his anxiety had been causing an audible buzz.

"Damn. I've never felt this good before without being

high . . ." Conner raised his eyebrows and relaxed fully into the chair.

"Ha! Good!" I laughed. "And do you see how easy that was?"

Conner nodded. Still smiling. Not totally in the room with me, but this time distant in peace instead of dissociated in shame and suffering.

I waited a bit before I asked Conner to rejoin me a little more fully by prompting him to notice his sensations again.

"Can you feel the chair under you? Try to notice again where the chair and your body connect. And maybe look around the room a little, just to bring you back here a bit more."

Conner looked around the room and took another long breath.

"Yeah. Wow. That's crazy. I feel like I'm actually here now. Weird. I don't think I've really totally been here before." Conner's eyes were wide.

"Let's take our time and move slowly then, okay? I'll start asking you some questions but notice if you get that floaty feeling of not being here and we'll pause. I don't want you to leave your body again."

Conner nodded. "Yeah, cool. I'm good."

I wanted to keep things simple and stay with his sensations to keep him grounded.

"Good. Okay."

I took a breath too and paused for just a bit longer.

"We've got lots of time left and I want to return to where we left off. I think we need to start figuring out what you actually like, and who you actually are," I told Conner. "We need to understand what a really good life would feel like for you."

For Conner, learning to listen to himself was going to require a *huge* shift. It meant practicing listening to his instincts, body, and the things that activated his joy, even when—especially when—they seemed to make no logical sense. It meant continuing to separate his sense of self from his parents' goals or desires for him. It meant shifting gears from everything he had worked for during high school and college, so that he could begin living according to his own goals for life, his own interests, most of which he could barely name or had refused to take seriously. It would probably mean, at some point, giving up the Adderall that I suspected he was abusing. I knew it was a process that would take years and hopefully continue for a lifetime.

But I wanted to find a relatively simple way for Conner to start.

"Do you remember Goldilocks?" I asked Conner.

"Goldilocks? Yeah . . ." He was skeptical.

"I think she needs to be your new teacher."

I knew I was being corny, but I needed an image that would stick.

"Wait. Why Goldilocks?"

"Do you remember her story? What was she like?"

"Too big, too small, just right," he responded.

"Exactly! Too hot, too cold, just right."

"So . . . what does that mean? What's the homework?"

"The homework is to do the same thing. Goldilocks tested things to clarify what felt right *for her*. It's subjective information. I encourage you to start noticing what actually brings you joy. Not just what you *think* brings you joy, or is *supposed* to bring you joy, but what actually does. You can also notice what you *don't* like."

Conner nodded, one hand resting softly on top of the other in his lap.

"You need to use your body and senses and imagination to actually *feel* what you like, what works for you personally. *For you.* As an individual. Not because of what you're told to like or not like. This means feeling it out for yourself."

Conner seemed to be trying to take in what I was saying. I wasn't sure how much was making sense. I continued, at the risk of overdoing it.

"Let me put it this way: You need to act like a toddler who just reaches for toys and foods and notices likes or dislikes, either reaching for more or spitting it out. I'd like you to practice returning to a time when you listened to your body and desires, before you knew anything about other people's perceptions and expectations for you. You'll want to kind of start following through on interests and curiosities, however small. Start feeling things out and see where it goes."

"Huh, okay." Conner made eye contact with me.

"Is this making sense?"

Conner nodded. "I think so."

Like the story of Goldilocks's physical testing of her environment, many Quarterlifers, particularly Stability Types, need to practice how to *feel* things out versus *figure* things out: too hot, too cold, *just right*; too small, too big, *just right*.

This Goldilocks method isn't interested in perfection or what others think. Symbolically, Goldilocks wanders into the

realm of her animal nature, the Bears' home, and begins testing her environment with her senses. As she sits in each chair
or tastes each bowl of porridge, she's focused on the rightness
for her of each thing. This Goldilocks method means allowing curiosity about everything from food to music to climates,
cities, ideas, authors, artwork, relationships, and communities.

Listening is a critical component of Quarterlife. I think it's
a part of the developmental journey that Carl Jung once considered a given: As Quarterlifers went into the world to find
out who they were, they would be guided by their instincts
and curiosities and gradually learn about themselves. But
since academia has extended the length of structured, external development well into people's twenties, the concept of
living guided by instinct has become undervalued and is now
just viewed as aimless wandering. This is why it was so important for Conner to adjust his plans, at least for a while.
Many Quarterlifers feel that they're on a moving sidewalk of
life, a path that is so predetermined in its journey—high
school, college, degree, job—that it carries each person along
with it, with or without conscious consent or interest. Even
when there are massive disruptions, the next goal is likely to
scramble to "get back on track." Practicing listening in
Quarterlife is changing the focus from achieving a goal to
indulging curiosity—in order to understand the path itself.
It's a practice of gathering information about one's own specific nature. Do I like this activity? Do I like time alone in the
mornings? How do I need to challenge myself to grow?
Whom do I admire for their character, and why? No one else
knows the answers to those questions.

Quarterlifers can only truly determine their experience of life through trial and error, so recognizing one's physical and emotional reactions in any given situation, even subtly, provides information. I encourage clients to listen for resistance, fear, longing, excitement, exhaustion, curiosity, and bashfulness when they arise. Before asking what any of it means, I suggest acting as a nature observer, simply attending to one's own experience in the world.

For a while, I didn't know how much Conner was taking in. I tried to explore his other likes and dislikes with him in our sessions, learning about the interests besides basketball he'd had as a child, and watching for when he perked up around anything we were discussing. We were both trying to "hear into" what attracted his interest, even when he didn't really know why. I wanted to support Conner's curiosity in himself through my curiosity in him. I soon learned, relieved, that it was working more than I'd realized.

Quieting the Noise

"I really do like looking at beautiful women," Danny mused one afternoon.

The Americano that had become his pre-therapy ritual was in his left hand in a sleek metal mug, his arm resting on the chair.

"I was waiting for my coffee outside and there were these two women who walked by, wearing these fitted business skirts. I loved just watching them walk . . ." Danny began to blush.

It had been many months since Danny had gone off his

medication for bipolar disorder. We barely ever spoke about the former diagnosis, though we did talk about his depression. His prescriber was still exploring the possibility of adding an antidepressant as well as getting his vitamin B12 levels checked. Danny's largely vegetarian diet made B12 depletion a good possibility, which was a danger for his emotional well-being. I also wanted to support Danny to develop greater discernment in witnessing when, specifically, he was lethargic, and if his lethargy had other roots that hadn't been identified. I encouraged Danny to hear into these experiences in order to gather information about what was going to help him truly thrive in the world, rather than just survive and get by. To start, I was curious to learn more about this attraction he'd just experienced at the coffee shop and the resulting energy he seemed to be feeling—caffeine aside.

Soon, Danny and I were digging deeper into areas of shame and discomfort that he hadn't wanted to discuss before, sex and sexuality among them. In addition to feeling physically unwell, Danny was sorting through questions of embodiment and masculinity at this moment in history. He had explored at times what it would feel like to live in the world as nonbinary and sometimes wrestled with his gender identity. But mostly, he just wondered what it would feel like to redefine what it meant to be male and heterosexual in the world and in a Latino family. There were a lot of layers of identity to unpack and explore.

"I feel like my father and uncles—even my grandfather—modeled for me a lot of the old stereotypes of *Latino* men, you know?"

"How so?" I asked.

"Just like the classic stuff around gender roles, like I'd get invited out to do things with my brothers when I was still young, to play baseball or whatever, and my sisters were expected to stay home. One of my sisters always wanted to join us and she just couldn't. And meanwhile I never really wanted to go play baseball, you know? I didn't care. We joked about wishing we could switch places. I really meant it."

Danny hadn't talked much about this part of his childhood before. I was learning a lot.

"It happened on my mom's side too. Her brothers, they're Cuban—my dad's side is Costa Rican—they'd do similar stuff. Like my sisters were really expected to be cooking and helping at parties and if I ever got up to help, they'd start teasing me, like it was emasculating to help my sisters. We just all got shoved into these stupid, stupid roles."

"It felt stifling." I reflected the underlying feeling of what he was describing.

"Really stifling," Danny agreed.

Increasingly, as Danny learned more and talked more about toxic masculinity, he shuddered at representations of it in the world and shrank at the idea that he could be a part of any of it. But the confusion around gender roles and how to "be a man" had become crippling. He was still sorting through what it meant to be male and proud of his body and his culture without perpetuating old myths around manhood.

I was about to return to what had kicked off this conversation when Danny got there first: "And yet here *I* am objectifying these women at the coffee shop as they're just walking by, living their lives!"

"Well . . ." I hesitated. "Hold on. There's nothing wrong

with finding people attractive. Why do you think you were objectifying them?"

"I don't know. Maybe I wasn't. I guess for a moment, it just felt good to really feel like, *'wow'* without the shame of that feeling showing up too. They were just both so beautiful, these two women walking by like *bosses*." Danny laughed and caught himself. "Oh my god. Isn't this weird that I'm talking like this with you?"

"No." I smiled. "Not at all. That's what we do here. Do you feel weird talking about it?"

"A little." He shrugged. "But not really, I guess . . ."

I waited.

"It's hard to explain," Danny mumbled as he shrank back into the chair.

"We've got tons of time," I told him. "No need to rush through anything."

"I need to tell you about something that I'm always scared to bring up."

"Okay," I began. "I'm ready to hear it."

Danny sighed, then rubbed his forehead and his scalp, a gold band and a beaded bracelet clanking together briefly on his wrist.

"Uck." He looked disgusted. "You sure? It's so weird. I mean, it's *weird*."

"I can handle it," I offered. "And if I'm uncomfortable for some reason, we'll talk about it, okay?"

"Okay."

I waited in silence as he got up the nerve to dive in.

"Okay, okay . . ." He paused, clearly just trying to blurt something out. "I think I'm addicted to porn."

This was the first time I'd heard Danny mention pornography. But I didn't feel surprised. Porn addiction is common for a generation of Quarterlifers raised on the Internet, in particular with parents and a whole society that have been slow to understand the level of accessibility to porn, or the degree to which the content is both explicitly erotic and regularly violent, exploitative, and humiliating in nature. I often see clients who have entered a classic trauma "freeze" state because of what they have seen, and then, with a mix of emotions, go back to see it again and again, as if craning to see a terrible car crash while still in shock. The blend of conscious and unconscious emotions can feel confusing, paralyzing, and shameful.

"Tell me more." I leaned in.

"I honestly think it started when I was like ten. Way too early. One of my uncles showed me some stuff in a magazine, and then I saw something online and just sort of fell down a rabbit hole."

I nodded again.

"It was so weird at the time, I remember. I was sort of scared at first but like really aroused too, you know?" He looked at me. "You're okay?"

"I'm okay." I smiled.

Danny took a deep breath.

"I think from then on it's been this difficult, confusing, back and forth thing. Like I want to stop watching it, but I'm—" He looked at the corner of the room. "I can't."

He was still deep in thought. We sat together in silence.

"I know it's connected to how I feel about sex and, ugh—" He paused. "And my body and being a man, or whatever.

Because the penises in porn are, like, so *intense*"—he paused again—"and so violent. The men can be so gross and cruel."

I continued in silence with him as he allowed these thoughts and feelings that had been wound up to unspool.

"It's, like, so weird to hate something ethically and be addicted to it too. I haven't been able to stop." He looked away with shame in his eyes. "I keep trying to stop." Danny sighed heavily and looked back at me as if to check again that I was okay—that *we* were okay and I hadn't suddenly changed my perception of him.

For Danny, learning to listen to himself meant improving his attention to his body and embodiment, rather than looking away. More specifically, this meant exploring the experience of being in a body that he'd long associated with overpowering, misogynistic, and violent sex. It's not the kind of sex that Danny consciously wanted, and he knew that men who look like him are often sexualized too, expected to be sexual and always desiring of women. He was trying to carefully tease apart what was true for him, what the result of a porn addiction was, and what were various cultures telling him what he was supposed to want and be.

Danny needed to understand his own individual self and desires, not those portrayed to him through outside sources. He knew he wasn't comfortable engaging in sex with women in the ways he'd seen in porn, ways he described as "hierarchical and performative." But he also really wasn't sure yet what he was comfortable with, which was part of the reason that dating had been so complicated for him. In a way, rather than explore sex and sexuality much at all, he'd just gotten trapped in ponderous thoughts in his head.

Learning to listen to his sensual self, his embodied self, would take time and patience. There was no single solution or method to help him resolve what needed to be resolved. It was a long process of self-discovery, of continuing to separate from past representations of masculinity in his family and in society that didn't feel right to him, while working to truly listen to his body and its reactions. It meant quieting the external noise that suggested he should like *this* or *that,* as well as turning down the noise of his addiction that was garbling his perceptions of women and of himself. For Danny, this increased pursuit of embodiment also meant gaining comfort with self-pleasure in ways that did not involve pornography or visual stimulation. It meant noticing organic arousal and delight, just as he had at the coffee shop. It meant enhancing the relationship with himself on his own.

Danny's journey toward quieting a lot of the extraneous noise included working through body-mind practices as well, including finding healers from various modalities who could support him. The process of allowing skilled practitioners to gently touch his body helped Danny to develop trust with himself, his body, and the physical, nonsexual presence of others. He also began attending yoga classes at a studio in his neighborhood. Though, at first, he felt incredibly awkward being on display in a room with people, he soon found a routine with it and one teacher with whom he felt particularly safe.

"Do you have some favorite postures yet?" I asked Danny one day as we were finishing our session and he was gathering his things.

He laughed. "For sure Savasana." Danny's eyes twinkled

as he referred to the end of class when students lie still in "corpse pose," a posture that stimulates the parasympathic nervous system, supporting healthy rest and digestion in the body.

"It's a pretty delicious moment when it arrives," I agreed.

"Honestly, I really love it because I can feel the energy moving through my body in a new way. It's like the opposite of pain. Like a pulsing energy sometimes that feels good instead of bad. You know?"

I nodded and smiled. "I do."

CHAPTER 8

Build

*What do you need to create, cultivate, or
construct in your life?*

The third pillar of growth is to "Build." The English, German, and Sanskrit verbs that mean "to build, construct, cultivate" are derived from root words meaning "to be, become, arise." To Build one's life is to become oneself. As a natural partner to the receptivity required of Listening, Building requires effort, consistency, and willpower.

Hard work has long been encouraged in Quarterlife—it's foundational to the "join the real world" admonishment. But the emphasis tends to be on universal developmental goals, becoming a functioning part of the social fabric and an economic contributor, rather than manifesting one's own *specific, individual* life. When we use a psychological, rather than an economic, lens on adulthood, the emphasis on effort turns toward creating a singular meaningful and stable life. Social participation remains vital, as does attention to survival and financial well-being. But it doesn't end there. Building one's life is about *consciously* crafting one's existence with hard work, love, and dedication. The opus of building one's specific life requires tiny and large labors, structures and order, and often a lot of faith and trust too.

Sometimes this work means taking seriously the desire to learn a new skill that requires a great deal of focus to pursue, like a martial art, a musical instrument, or how to make hand-thrown pottery. It could also be something as practical as emphasizing daily meal planning. Or it could mean something relational, like actively pursuing dating and communication rather than just waiting for chance encounters or passive conflict resolution. The goals may also be much larger in scope, like applying to an academic program or training for an athletic competition. Depending on the Quarterlifer, these goals will support building greater meaning in one's life, building necessary structures of stability—or both.

An emphasis on building the life one wants requires consistency, focus, and pushing through fatigue or internal limitations. It often involves long-term commitments to tasks in order to counteract a lack of faith in one's self, a lack of trust in the possibility of a better life, or a persistent struggle to manifest one's desired future. Often the work required to build one's life and future is monotonous and difficult—but it is this work that may truly bring change and transform an entire personality too.

The theme of monotonous labor shows up symbolically in fairy tales and myths. Certainly, when it comes to willpower, there are images of perseverance, bravery, and acts of warrior strength, like the twelve labors of Hercules in which the hero accomplished seemingly impossible feats such as killing menacing beasts, stealing prized golden apples from Zeus, and cleaning vast animal stables in a day. When not driven by fear of punishment, such efforts can be critical for growth: transforming laziness and dependence into confidence and self-reliance. But images of hard work often come in much smaller, more methodical and mundane packages, as in the story of "Eros and Psyche" by Apuleius, in which Psyche is separated from her great love, Eros, and is forced to perform impossibly dull and monotonous tasks in order to reunite with him. In one task forced upon her by the goddess Venus, Psyche needs to sort tiny grains and beans, one by one, from where they are mixed together in one huge pile. A very similar theme appears in the original Cinderella story. Before Cinderella could go to the royal ball to meet the prince, she had to remove individual lentils from the ashes in the fireplace where her stepmother had thrown them. At first, both Psyche and Cinderella despaired. But in both cases, their instincts eventually awakened, embodied by the arrival of ants and birds that helped them to accomplish their work. Both Psyche and Cinderella finished the once seemingly impossible tasks, and both found their ways toward reunion, an integration, with their other half.

Adventure and risk-taking can be critical parts of Quarterlife, but the inner and outer work of building one's life often feel more like these repetitive tasks than classic adventure stories. Through careful attention to building the life one wants, piece by exhausting piece, Quarterlifers create new boundaries, learn new skills, and gain resilience along the way. Through it all, one's identity and personality are molded and formed, and a deeply rooted self-respect is won.

Developing a Discipline

"I need to get serious about my writing," Danny told me one afternoon. "I'm still pretty sure that it's a huge waste of my time, but I'm not doing anything else." He shrugged and slumped in the chair, crossing his ankles out in front of him. It was winter and his jeans, apropos of his style, seemed a couple inches too short. His socks were mismatched.

"What are you planning to work on?" I asked.

"My short stories," he began. "I want to get at least five done. Really done. I need to be able to talk to editors about them without making excuses or sounding like that annoying kid who thinks he's going to be a great writer someday, but won't even sit down to do it. It's the only thing anyone tells you: If you want to be a writer, you have to write."

"It's true," I agreed.

Danny grabbed a bright sweatshirt out of his bag and slipped it over his shoulders before picking up the coffee he'd placed down.

Now that Danny had been practicing listening more to his own physical desires and needs to heal from his past, he felt a visceral need to build his future too, to bring something—and himself—into form. While listening requires deep attention to oneself and nonverbal cues, building is a much more tangible undertaking.

"I'm thinking of setting a schedule for myself," Danny continued. "I feel like the main thing now is that I need to be honest about my energy. I go into these manic bursts where I'll stay up all night writing, but then I just burn out and it can be weeks before I come back to it."

"You want a consistent writing schedule so you don't burn out," I reflected, simply.

"Yeah, like something realistic that works for me. It's not like I'm going to start writing in the morning or anything." I knew that Danny was not a morning person. "But I think finding what actually works for a writing schedule in the late afternoons and evenings makes sense."

Danny hadn't had a model for this kind of consistency and focus in his childhood. His parents had worked hard, and constantly, but not in support of their own creative lives. Danny's mother had exhibited a relentless work ethic, but one that almost intimidated Danny with its self-denial. His stepfather was similar. Danny's father, meanwhile, had always displayed a more chaotic lifestyle along with a brimming but unused creativity. Danny was still learning to believe that manifesting his own writing and creativity was possible. Believing in an alternate future that was neither stressful nor riddled with self-denial was a form of re-parenting.

We were also working together on detoxing from the harmful and pervasive message that to be a creative person means you have to be unhealthy, stoned, or drunk. Deconstructing this story is often critical for Meaning Types in particular, who can feel that if they give up their unhealthy patterns, they'll lose their creativity too.

"Do you think you can write after you get back from work?" I asked.

Danny worked four days a week at a pet supply store.

"Yeah, I mean, it's much easier than in the mornings before I leave. I know it's going to be hard to switch gears after work. But I have to."

For many Meaning Types like Danny, building the life they want often requires an almost spiritual devotion to consistency, a dedication to what often feel like "mundane" or "pointless" tasks but is ultimately a long-term effort to enhance their stability in the world. While some love "the grind" and the feeling that they're finally creating something, others worry that they're "selling out" or becoming "normal." These notions speak to another underlying fear that haunts Meaning Types: If they commit fully to life, they'll become soulless and without personality, like human drones. In many ways, this is how Danny perceived his parents' relationship to work. So he needed to understand that the focus on consistency and stability, however mundane it might feel, could be oriented toward manifesting his own life, not just society's expectations for him to perform for the economy and survive.

Often what starts as a devotion to routine can awaken embodied instincts that ultimately make daily life more functional and less difficult. The ritual of building evokes stories of great musicians and artists who commit to laboriously learning classic techniques for years before they are able to begin truly *playing* with their form. I think of the Karate Kid, whose wise instructor insists that he methodically wax a car—"wax on, wax off"—in order to learn, unwittingly, the exacting karate postures that he craves to know. Dedication to the right forms and process of one's art, however boring it is at first, can make space for something new and brilliant to emerge.

This consistent practice can also be a psychological necessity. For Meaning Types, the emphasis on building one's life is like finding an island in a wide-open ocean after floating aimlessly without sight of land; it is a reliable place to dry out and experience stability where there was previously just chaos, depression, or overwhelm.

Danny did start writing regularly. Sometimes he'd fall asleep at his desk, and have to try again the next day. In these moments, he'd descend into a shame spiral about how "dumb" he was or how "absurd" his goals were. There were plenty of days and evenings that felt painful. An endless slog. But he kept trying. This return to the work, even when he desperately wanted to give up, was key. He was building his own resilience through devotion, and he began to feel an instinctual love of sitting at his desk, regardless of how productive he ended up being. By showing up to write, even when he felt anxious, he was proving himself to himself.

"I've started looking forward to it," Danny told me some months later. "It's become like my nest or something." He smiled at the thought as he stretched his arms high above his head. "I just sort of curl up there with my tea and my little lamp. I light a candle and some incense. And then I just stay and work."

"That sounds lovely," I reflected.

I knew too that Danny had placed images of some of his favorite thinkers around his desk like an altar of elders, an exercise that we'd talked about for inspiration. I imagined these individuals—Octavia Butler, Roberto Bolaño, Ursula K. Le Guin, and others—staring back at him as he worked. These were writers who had their own share of struggles. Writers who brought their work into the world despite countless odds. For Danny, the effort of building meant a determination to grow toward these people. They were like wise guides who helped him to stay focused night after night.

Everything about Danny's life began to orient around this new determination to write, like the lives of new parents orient around their newborn baby. By necessity, his structure included setting multiple boundaries and decreased socializing. Danny's mini writing retreat each evening meant that he had to learn to say no to friends on a regular basis, honoring his self-care and goals above the needs of others.

"I think I'm working best from like 8 to 11 P.M. or so." He shrugged. "I'm really trying to commit to putting in three hours a day—or night—for at least a year. I started this a couple of weeks ago and it's going well so far."

"Every day?"

"Yeah, I mean, I know I need to take days off sometimes, and that's okay. Maybe Fridays every week. Maybe Fridays and Sundays. We'll see. But for the most part it feels good to be this focused. There's a schedule to everything at the moment: when I eat, sleep, walk, see friends."

This work to build his life began to support Danny to tend to his physical needs too. If Danny was truly going to write, he knew that he had to attend fully to what he was eating, how often he was walking or going to yoga, and when he slept. The structure Danny was building was ultimately a foundation for life in general that he'd desperately needed.

Many Quarterlifers feel, instinctively, that they're not pushing themselves hard enough, like there's an invisible inner hurdle that they need to overcome as much as there are external obstacles to be pushed through. Danny struggled with this feeling all the time, trying to discern what was his own laziness or physical fatigue, and what was pure avoidance at any given moment. He needed to practice pushing himself just like a parent pushes their child when they're learning to ride a bike. Good parenting includes knowing when to say "try again," despite the tears and the scraped knees. This is what Danny was learning to do for himself.

Getting Practical

"This is so hard," Grace began one afternoon, sitting down as if collapsing. "I don't know if I can do this alone."

"What do you mean by 'this'?" I asked, gently.

"Life . . . life, I guess." Her anxious breathing began to give way to tears. I knew that Grace often stored things up through the week for our hour together and hoped, for her sake, that she hadn't been like this for days. "I don't understand how people handle everything they need to handle without just feeling overwhelmed all the time."

"What are you overwhelmed by right now? What in particular?"

"Rent. Food. Money." She was panicking. "How do people handle paying for things they need!?"

I took a deep breath to model for her what her body needed. I asked her to do the same. She did. We started to slow things down a little.

"Your income isn't enough to pay for what you need?" I asked quietly. I was still trying to understand what had catalyzed this particular bout of fear.

"I don't even know, is the thing. I just have my bank account and my credit cards. I got a medical bill that I can't even open. It's just sitting in my kitchen. I threw out a stack of other envelopes before I moved."

"Is that part of what kicked off your anxiety this week? Getting that medical bill?"

Grace began sputtering tears, her chest rising and falling in irregular bursts. "Yes." She barely got the word out of her mouth. "Yes!"

I sat with her in silence for a while, letting her cry and release the stress that she'd been carrying. Then she began to calm a bit. It was helpful to localize the total overwhelm she'd been feeling to a single, identifiable cause.

"How do people handle all of this?" she asked me again, more rhetorically now.

"It can be a lot sometimes, there's no question. Wages are too low and there's very little support for Quarterlifers to tackle all of this stuff at once," I began. "It sucks."

Grace nodded. "Yeah. It sucks. I can't even imagine having student debt like some of my friends."

"I know," I replied. "It's a lot." We sat in silence again as she wiped her eyes and started to breathe more regularly.

"Can we get into the details a bit more? I'd like to understand more clearly what you're dealing with."

Grace nodded and brushed a few short wisps of platinum blond hair from her eyes; her nails were covered with chipped pink polish.

"How about you bring that envelope into our next session? Bring all of the mail you're scared to open?"

"There are voicemails too."

"Voicemails? That you can't listen to?"

"Yeah, I have like twenty voicemails that I haven't listened to."

"Okay, can we start there, then?"

"Now?" She looked at me hesitantly.

I nodded.

She sighed as she leaned toward her messenger bag to grab her phone. She pulled it out, unlocked it, stared at the screen, and started crying again.

"There are thirty-three!" She raised her eyebrows at me. "Thirty-three!"

"Okay, no one has died, though . . . I don't think, anyway." I winked. Her self-hatred around "not being a successful adult" was only going to undermine her more if I didn't defuse the panic a bit, practically and playfully. "Go ahead . . ." I gestured with my head for her to continue.

Grace sighed and pressed play. The first message was a few seconds long and static. The second and third were robocalls. She deleted all of them.

"The next three are from Josie," she told me. Josie was a close friend. "They're from two months ago!"

"Have you seen her since then?"

Grace laughed. "I've probably seen her every day since then."

"I guess it can't be that bad then!"

Grace pressed play on those messages too. All three were Josie screaming and laughing into the phone. Drunk dials.

"So . . . ? How's this going so far?" I teased Grace.

"It's not so scary!" She giggled. "I'll do the rest later."

"Okay, how about you check them as soon as you leave, so they don't keep hanging over you like they have been."

"Okay, yeah. I will."

"And if you find anything scary or overwhelming, maybe you can bullet point them and send me an email?"

"Sure."

"And you'll bring the mail in next week?"

Grace nodded.

Over a year of hard healing work and learning to listen to herself, Grace's primary emphasis on building her future began to center around basic life logistics and facing what often felt like an onslaught of communication from people she loved. In addition to dealing with unanswered voicemails and text messages, Grace brought in the letter about her medical debt. Then we looked at her credit card bills, talked about the APR rates, and brainstormed ways that she could lower her debt most effectively. As I learned more about her financial situation, I encouraged Grace to print off three months of her bank statements and use a highlighter to color-code her different types of expenses: food, rent, transportation, beauty, clothes, etc. She took to this practice easily and repeated it on her own a few months later to see what had changed.

I'm not a financial planner or a budgeting expert. But unfortunately, this type of assistance with money is often inaccessible for my clients, so I don't like to avoid the issue when they're struggling with finances, just as I don't want to avoid discussions around sex, addictions, or trauma. I start where my clients are and consider all of life's content as material for therapy. Finances, in addition to other "life skills" like cooking, cleaning, hygiene, and paperwork, are all up for exploration. We're typically picking up where society, schools, and parents left off.

A lot of this work that might get woven into Quarterlife therapy is now popularly referred to as "adulting." It's the skills and knowledge that were once tied to heteronormative gender roles: Girls were taught that their jobs would be cleaning, housekeeping, childcare, and cooking; boys learned that their jobs would be to make money and provide for the family, skills they'd often learn on the job. Social expectations for Quarterlifers have transformed dramatically (thank goodness), but cultural support has not caught up. What practical knowledge may once have been passed down through a same-sex parent, family, or peers in the past is no longer shared in the same way. And while everyone is encouraged to go to school and get an education, the majority of that education is irrelevant to day-to-day life and survival. The vacuum of information around basic life skills can be massive.

This is all practical stuff, but when approached in a certain way, it also lends itself to psychological growth. Building structure can make the difference between a stressful life and a joyful one. An emphasis on simplifying confusing life skills can provide tremendous self-confidence for Meaning Types. For Grace, creating space for a meticulous attention to finances became a critical component of therapy. As Grace began to feel like she *did* have the capacity to understand and deal with her finances, she began to feel less hopeless and "childish" in life in general. By emphasizing money and finances, Grace was building her other half, her Stability self, the vehicle for her life. She was building her surfboard to gain more control in the waves.

"I called all my credit card companies yesterday about lowering my interest rates," Grace announced one day. She was holding her color-coded bank and credit card statements in her hand shortly after our session began. "I wanted to make sure I did it before our appointment so we could talk about it."

"And how'd it go?" I asked, impressed that she'd made those calls without a pep talk in advance.

"They both lowered the rates for me!" She felt so victorious. "I mean, I was on hold *forever,* but it worked! They actually lowered the rates!"

"That's amazing!"

"But one of them is still way higher than the other one, so I'm going to pay that one off first. I think I can do it by the end of this year. That will feel good . . ."

I smiled, delighted.

I knew that none of this was easy. Grace was making very little money at her job, and she also accrued debt with me from time to time, for her insurance co-pays. She had a lot to tackle. But realizing that she could learn this stuff was liberating for her. It no longer felt like an impenetrable realm that only certain people could access. She knew that the more of these skills she could learn, the less she'd feel desperate for support from others in the way she once had. She was demystifying the world and learning how far she could dream.

Our shared goals were not for Grace "to grow up" and "get real"—how anyone thinks a struggling Quarterlifer is going to eagerly step into life with that sales pitch is inconceivable to me. No one wants to "join the real world" if all that means is taxes and stress. The goal in building stability for Meaning Types like Grace has to be personal, evocative of growth and transformation. Once Grace was able to see the value in improving her relationships with money and daily tasks, they stopped exhausting her the way they had. Instead, this work began to feel like part of her larger pursuit of independence. Grace had always believed deeply in other people's capacity to grow and live good lives, and now she was beginning to truly believe in her own capacity to do the same.

(De)Constructing One's Life

"How's it been so far?" I asked Mira shortly after she arrived.

She grimaced a bit at my question. In general, Mira had been feeling much better. Our sessions had been helping her to tap into a part of herself that she'd repressed for years, for almost as long as she could remember. In general, her demeanor had brightened and she felt more playful to me; less rigid, more open. But today, Mira looked rather miserable.

"It's been hard, honestly."

Mira had finally committed to taking an extended break from work. She was using some of the two hundred hours of vacation time she'd accumulated, and was tacking on unpaid time off as well. After a lot of preparation, she spoke with her boss and received his blessing. She had plans for how she'd use her time away that felt inspiring to her, and relieving. But this was the first week of her break and it didn't seem to be going as she'd hoped.

"I'm already not meditating in the mornings like I'd planned. I'm just feeling lost all day." She sighed. "I'm already thinking about going back to work early."

Mira's doubt filled the room. I suddenly worried that maybe this break had been a mistake. Maybe it wasn't what she needed. But I struggled to imagine that work was what she needed either.

"Tell me more," I encouraged.

Mira shrugged. I waited with her as she sorted through her thoughts.

"I think I'm just really uncomfortable without structure. I feel anxious at home. I mean, I'm not totally lost. I'm cooking a lot more and working through my mother's recipes, which feels good. But there's a lot of time that is just *open*."

"It feels too unstructured."

Mira nodded. "I've always done better with deadlines and meeting expectations, honestly." She paused for a long while. "I think Tom's already worried too."

"Tom's worried?"

"Yeah. He knows how I normally am on weekends. I'm just so lazy and tired. He's afraid I'm going to turn into that person all the time, become a couch potato and get depressed. He knows I don't have many hobbies and that I'm not, honestly, very self-motivated at all."

"So you think he's right?"

"I think there's a good chance," Mira conceded.

She began biting her bottom lip with her front teeth in a small, nervous repetition, which seemed to stall her breathing. She looked like she was physically bracing herself. Without work, it was like she was going through withdrawal.

For Stability Types like Mira who have built a great deal of structure in their life, engaging with the pillar of Building may actually need to begin with demolition: deconstructing the safety and security that already exists but is not serving one's Meaning in any way. Mira had built a functional life. It was a good life. But lately, her internal desires for something more had become impossible to ignore. Once basic survival needs have been met, the function of stability is to serve meaning. Whether it's a house to provide for the kids and activities that one enjoys, or a job that makes adventures, volunteering, and a healthy life possible, at some point, meaning has to become the core focus. If stability remains the focus of one's life long after daily survival has been achieved, life is likely to start to feel empty sooner than later. This is where Mira had been, and she needed to carefully deconstruct the life that she'd built, almost like breaking down a theater set after a long production, before she could build another one. This was a massive reorientation. I tried to remind her of this.

"How about just letting yourself sleep in for a while? Maybe writing down your dreams in the morning instead of trying to get up at a set time to meditate, or to do anything that feels strict with yourself."

"Yeah," Mira agreed. "I know. I'm really kind of useless right now. The reality is that I'm sleeping in anyway, I'm just mad that I am. Or I get up when Tom does so he doesn't think I'm being lazy. Then I just go back to bed again and feel bad about myself."

"I think you could use a proper break."

After working so hard, Mira agreed that some sluggish time at home, without any motivation, could be expected and should be fully embraced. We discussed how she might convey to her husband what she really needed for these first few weeks, in order to address his concerns and make sure she had space. We talked about how it was okay for her to just lie around, listening to music or a podcast, or to read a few good novels back-to-back. Her imagination needed a reboot. We also knew there was a fine line between slowing down and checking out. So we talked about the importance of her limiting time online and with social media, and she agreed that she'd delete all of her accounts from her phone so she wouldn't get sucked into a black hole of scrolling. She understood that, in addition to some time to detox from work, what she really needed was unstructured time to allow something new to emerge.

"I need to just *get* that the goal is different now."

"Say more." I was curious.

"Like instead of the goal being to hit a deadline or make a client happy, it's . . ." She paused, thinking. "The goal would be to see what Mirabai feels like doing or what Jennifer is *scared* to do, and then to move in that direction to stretch her limits."

"You're amazing." I smiled. "Yes. That."

"It's like Jennifer needs to get out of the driver's seat and release control. And Mirabai needs to learn to take the helm."

For Stability Types, after some deconstruction, building their true life is a nuanced affair. It's a process that forces them to orient away from the expectations (or perceived expectations) of others, and toward their own self and interests, however unclear at first. This work requires a constant checking back in with their bodies and souls, a regular return to listening for guidance, and then a commitment to implementation. It's a radical act of *trusting*: trusting that their soul-self might be right, even when others don't understand, or when it's in opposition to the status quo. This was very true for Mira.

It took time. She had to continually push back against the inner doubt that this break was all wrong and that she should go back to work. She needed to lean into the uncertainty and fear, and into the empty space in her days in which she could create something new.

"Speaking of Mirabai," I began slowly. I knew I was prodding a bit. "Have you thought about painting during this time . . . ?"

"Yes," she mumbled. "I know. I have thought a lot about painting. It's seriously bizarre how resistant to painting I am. I do not want to even think about it for some reason."

"Because part of you *really* wants to paint?"

"Yeah . . . I mean . . . yeah. It's like, I still cannot for the life of me figure out what *the point is,* which makes me not want to do it. But at the same time I also feel like I'll never want to stop painting if I start. It's weirdly scary."

"Jennifer and Mirabai are fighting." I smiled.

Mira shrugged and smiled. "I guess. And Jennifer's winning, huh?"

"But you really want to paint."

"Yeah . . ." Mira looked at me and then at her hands. She started biting her cheek and took a deep breath.

This was part of the test for Mira. Would she be able to

implement what her soul-self, Mirabai, was requesting—even pleading for at times? Would she allow the radical shift toward trusting this part of herself that was calling for attention, without needing to understand "the point"? This wasn't just an obligation that was driving her, but something deeply and uniquely *her*. It was a different, riskier taskmaster. Instead of work deadlines and client demands, this was a subtle, insistent inner *want*.

"I have been looking at painting supplies," Mira began again as if telling me a dangerous secret. "Honestly, I have a whole list of supplies I want to buy. I've been creating a list for a long time."

"Oh yeah?"

"Yeah. I've also emailed this guy about a studio space I found."

"You *have*?"

Mira nodded, but just looked down at her hands.

"Is it too scary to talk more about yet?"

She nodded again.

Rising from the Ashes

"I actually hated being on my basketball team," Conner announced one day, about six months into our meetings. He blurted this out as if he'd never said it aloud before and was forcing himself to tell me.

"Really?" I was genuinely surprised.

Conner shrugged a yes. He'd only ever spoken about basketball and his teammates with affection or when drenched in the tremendous shame of having "failed them."

"I mean, I love playing basketball," he started again, clarifying his point. "I'm a point guard." Conner looked at me, switching tones. "Do you know what a point guard is?"

I watch most of the local NBA Trail Blazers' games. I nodded to Conner's question and named our point guards.

"Right." He nodded. "I mean, I'm not like them, but I'm good. The feeling of hitting shots . . . it's hard to describe. Sometimes I feel like I'm almost a sniper. Everything I do is about precision. I love that. That focus on accuracy."

My ears pricked up hearing this. Conner had just expressed loving something. Something specific. I was still listening for those moments, learning about the nuances of Conner's interests. So much information about a person is found in the details of what they love, and why.

"You love the feeling of precision," I reflected.

"Yeah. I love the feeling of the ball leaving my fingers, pretty much knowing already whether or not it's going in." Conner's affect had changed as his body remembered those sensations. His skin brightened. "It's a great feeling," he mused.

But as Conner sat with that thought for a bit, something else arose, like he'd remembered how this conversation had started and what he'd wanted to share.

"I hated traveling for games, though. I always returned from games feeling completely depleted. It's like I'd rather play ball on my own. Just on the court at home by myself."

"You did that a lot growing up?"

"Oh yeah, every day after school and sometimes until it got dark."

I watched him remembering the comfort of shooting hoops on his own. Then his look darkened again.

"What was that?" I asked. "What did you just think about?"

"I can't stand my coach."

"Your college coach?"

"Yeah. I guess he's not my coach anymore . . . he was a bastard."

"How so?"

"In every way." Conner laughed. "He'd yell at us all the time, but, like, not the way you're supposed to as a coach. It was really sick sometimes."

Conner was still sorting through what had led him to drop out of school—the accidental demolition of his former life. He was picking up the pieces now and looking for answers, clarifying what had happened and what he wanted *now*. Little by little, he was working toward building a new life from the ashes.

"Also, while we're talking about this, I think I was in the wrong major."

"Oh yeah? Say more."

"The Comm Department is just where they put the athletes," Conner continued, reflecting on the Communications courses he'd been taking. "It all seemed completely pointless. It wasn't hard for me to get good grades, but I felt like an idiot the whole time 'cause it was all so easy. So dumb."

"You're getting clear on a lot."

Conner nodded again. He looked thoughtful.

"If I'm gonna go back to school, I have to make some changes." He looked me in the eye.

In addition to his increased clarity, I noticed that there was a significant difference in Conner's overall comportment in this session. He was "denser" in a way that I often notice with clients but find hard to explain. It was like he was more physically present as well as more mature and self-aware. I wondered what, in particular, had changed, and what he might have been doing differently.

"You feel much more here with me today," I began. "And you seem to be thinking clearly about a lot of stuff."

"I do feel better."

"Do you know what has changed?"

"Well, this entire week, I've been getting up at 9 A.M. and making myself breakfast."

I raised my eyebrows. "Yeah?"

"Yeah." Conner nodded, not conveying much enthusiasm but not disagreeing.

"And you've noticed it's made a difference in how you feel?"

"Ohhh yeah," he exclaimed, laughing a little.

"You really do *look* like you feel better."

I had tried to ask Conner about his relationship to food many months before, but this had always been a complex topic.

"Can we just check in about how well you're eating?" I'd asked back then. In that particular session, he'd appeared entirely zoned out and barely able to stay present to what I was asking.

"Eating?" he'd responded, confused.

"Yes, eating. Like, are you putting food into your body every day?"

Conner's lips spread out like he'd just been caught in an unsavory situation, his top and bottom teeth visible.

"Uhh. Not really?"

"Yeah." I nodded sadly. "I didn't think so."

For months following, I'd tried to weave in some education on nutrition into our sessions. Building an independent and satisfying life for himself would mean taking responsibility for his own basic needs, at least.

Diagnosable eating disorders are not uncommon in Quarterlife, but forms of disordered eating are almost ubiquitous. For a large variety of reasons—whether it's lack of money, lack of access to good food, limited training in food preparation, the cultural shift toward packaged, processed, non-nutritious food, or the opposite trend toward an obsession with purity and wellness—I would guess that the majority of Quarterlifers struggle in some way with food and eating.

"It sort of started for practical reasons," Conner had told me, about why he wasn't eating. "I think I was trying to save my parents money. And having Adderall helped a lot with the hunger. Sometimes I rail it too," he'd finally admitted, looking up at me, explaining how he would grind the pills into a powder to snort it.

"How often?" I'd asked.

"Every morning?" He'd paused and looked at his hands. "Sometimes in the afternoon too."

This had helped to explain at least some of Conner's visible exhaustion and his sunken, pale look. It also explained why his clothes often looked way too big and hung off his limbs. Conner had had a prescription for Adderall since early in high school. In college, he used it for performance enhancement, but since being home, he'd been using it much more just to numb his hunger or get going in the morning. I'd learned over time to recognize when Conner was subsisting almost entirely on uppers because of the angry look in his eyes and the persistence of his depression. He would often lash out at me in our sessions, like a depleted animal protecting a wound. I'd encourage Conner to grab some food right after we finished, knowing that if he went straight home he'd skip another meal.

It's worth noting that the pills that were making Conner crash to the point of suicidal ideation were prescribed and covered by insurance. The energy drinks that he'd sometimes bring to session were marketed directly to his demographic. Meanwhile, the food that he needed to keep his blood sugar regulated, his vitamin and pH levels balanced, and his body and mind functioning were less easily accessible and not marketed in his direction, nor swiftly consumed. This is core to the great irony and danger of modern Quarterlife psychology. What is helpful is often not socially encouraged, financially accessible, backed by effective advertising, nor supported by mainstream psychiatry, which tends to reach for diagnoses and pills while overlooking the importance of basic nutrition, moderate exercise, relationships, and regular sleep.

But today, in session, something about Conner was different. I was relieved to see him looking so much better. He suddenly seemed committed to rebuilding his life. He seemed ready to work on creating new structures and habits that could provide him the support he really needed.

"So, what did you make for breakfast?" I asked him.

"A big hash with potatoes, cheese, and spinach and some eggs on top." He looked up at me, a bit proud. "It was gooood." He laughed, drawing out the word for emphasis.

"It sounds good." I laughed along with him. I was comforted to see him so vibrant.

"I'm looking forward to getting some Thai food for dinner before I head back home too."

"That place around the corner is great." I gestured out the window.

"Yeah . . ." Conner nodded, seemingly mid-thought. "I've also been wanting to tell you . . . I quit using Adderall."

"Oh yeah?"

"Yeah. I finished the bottle last week and I'm not going to get my prescription filled again. I know it's not been good for me for a long time."

The shift toward creating new patterns in his life had taken root in private. I had struggled to know how much of our work was resonating with Conner, but somewhere it had clicked. He'd begun to clarify what wasn't healthy for him and was making changes. Bit by bit, like old toys or paperwork that he no longer needed, Conner discarded the college basketball team, the Communications major, and the Adderall. In recognizing this, he finished the deconstruction of the former structures and influences that were failing to provide him with a life he wanted to live. He was beginning now, in small ways, to build a life for himself that felt good.

CHAPTER 9

Integrate

*Can you step toward what's new and celebrate
what is coming to fruition?*

Psychological growth is rarely linear in the way that book chapters are. The often exquisitely difficult work of self-creation is complex and circular. In our growth, we each return over and over again to patterns we think we've healed and insights we've had before. This is why the four pillars are *pillars* that anchor growth, and not steps or stages. Moving through the work to Separate, Listen, and Build can feel more like an oscillation, or like weaving, as we move back and forth and back again. When an emphasis on building goes too far into an obsession to change things, for instance, a return to listening to one's self is often required. Similarly, when it becomes overly confusing to listen for one's own wants and needs, it's valuable to revisit separating inner voices from those of friends, former caretakers, or social norms in order to identify what's causing the complication. Over time, fresh patterns are created between the pillars like a beautifully formed web as the work to Separate, Listen, and Build begin to "Integrate" and together manifest something entirely new.

Integration may arrive with surprising and tangible "wins": success in one's career, creative work coming to fruition, or a glowing romantic connection that hadn't previously seemed possible. For many Quarterlifers, Integration can feel like magic when it occurs. Through big and small moments of culmination, there's a sense of symbiosis between one's soul-self and one's ego-self, an experience of one's inner and outer worlds coming into alignment. No longer at odds, one's Meaning-self and one's Stability-self are connected and *in relationship* in one's life.

After all the hard work to Separate, Listen, and Build, the ability to Integrate it all is a blessing. These experiences allow Quarterlifers to feel like they are truly part of the world, and part of world-making, rather than a mere bystander observing events or missing out on the action. For Quarterlifers who struggle to believe that something wonderful can arise after all the disorientation and pain they've endured, I emphasize that *loving one's life is possible,* and that the capacity to indulge joy and trust in good things is just as important as the difficult work that has come before. Taking the step to embrace integration means facing fears of vulnerability, intimacy, creativity, and success. It requires courage to become something different from what one was before, to trust a new path that feels exciting, and to choose one's own singular life.

A New Beginning

"I think all the paperwork is done now." After a year of working together, Conner was finalizing his plans to go back to college. The next semester started in a few weeks.

"Good work!" I smiled back at him.

"I think my parents are relieved that I'm going back," he began. "But . . . I told them that I've been in touch with my coach." He glanced at me quickly then away.

"You haven't been?"

"No. There's no way. There's no way I can play for him again."

"Are you going to tell them?"

"I have to, I guess. But I figured I'd start with the basics and get their help with enrolling in school again. First things first, you know?"

I understood the conundrum he was in, trying to balance the separation from his parents' expectations and hopes for him while developing the skill of self-trust. None of it was easy, especially as he was still quite financially dependent on his parents, a frequent point of Quarterlife complication.

Conner was still eating much better than he had been and had started to shoot hoops again at home most days. He knew that he felt familiar to his parents again. They didn't know everything that was going on inside of him, but he was at least someone they recognized.

"We don't talk about anything much, you know, but they've definitely backed off. They're not tracking me and worrying anymore."

Conner was consistently mellow when I saw him now, not as angry or amped up as he used to be. He didn't seem to be caught in iron-tight cycles of shame and self-loathing, and his self-care had improved dramatically. His Goldilocks investigations had borne tremendous fruit too.

"I've talked with an adviser at school about starting pre-med next semester," Conner shared.

"Oh, yeah?" We hadn't spoken much about science or medicine, but I've seen many times how the things that make people light up the most are often things they've struggled to even notice themselves. "Tell me more."

"I've been doing that thing of paying attention to what I like. I know that I don't like anything I've been learning in my classes so far, I know that I got sleepy in class all the time 'cause I was so bored. But I remembered this anatomy class that my coach had us take. I was so, so curious about it. My teammates were always teasing me because I raised my hand so much."

I smiled imagining him that vibrant and inquisitive.

"I want something that is applicable, you know? I've been thinking about how I love the accuracy of basketball, and the physical experience of it. I want that. Like I want to know the point of what I'm doing, and how to do it."

I was impressed by how deeply he was contemplating each of these pieces. I leaned forward, taking it all in.

"I mean, I know it'll be really hard. But I should explore the possibility anyway, right?"

"If it excites you, for sure. You're still in college."

"Yeah. I realized too that I kept thinking about this thing that happened a few years ago. I was driving with my high school coach senior year and we watched a car crash right in front of us. After we had pulled over, I jumped out and ran straight to the crash to see if people were okay." Conner paused. "I mean, I didn't really think about it. It was really bad, though. We stayed until the EMTs arrived and I was so relieved, sort of, to see them working."

"You could imagine yourself in that role," I reflected, hearing into what he was saying.

"I could, or I guess I was curious about it. I remembered that when I got back into the car, Coach said that the way I responded and engaged made him think I'd make a really good doctor. He said I was good under pressure and that I hadn't been scared off."

"Absolutely. That makes sense to me. I think part of what you loved about being a point guard was the pressure too, yeah?"

"Yeah, for sure." Conner nodded, energized.

"So what did the adviser say about it? Is it possible at this point for you to switch majors?"

"Yeah, so we talked about what it would take to do pre-med at this point. They're looking into it. I think it would mean at least another semester before I can graduate. Like an additional semester to what I already need to make up. But I did take some of the courses already, it turns out. So maybe it's worth it."

Conner was much closer to understanding what a life with both stability and meaning would look like for him. He was just twenty-one now. He'd still be sorting through how to separate himself from his parents and peer groups for years, clarifying his own perspectives and identity. If medical school was in his future, he'd have to work hard to stay connected to his body and build healthy routines. For Conner, learning to integrate all of the pieces was key. He needed to practice coming back to the self-awareness and rigor of self-care when he forgot, to work on communication with his parents and partners, and to allow himself to pursue true joy, even when it seemed scary, put him at odds with his folks, or made him an outsider for a time.

Conner adjusted his baseball cap in a couple of swift motions, up and down off his head. He cracked his knuckles and took a deep breath, a breath that actually moved through his body and didn't seem constrained by stress. His throat no longer tightened against every stray thought like a hungry snake. Conner appeared comfortable in his own skin, and his energy felt authentic and fluid, like a continuously moving river, instead of jarring and erratic.

"Is it weird that, after everything, I'm actually sort of excited about going back to school?" Conner asked, looking straight at me as his question hung in the air.

"No." I beamed.

Conner knew me well enough now to know what I meant with just one word. I had worked to normalize his pain and confusion, to teach him about self-care, to de-pathologize every psychological symptom he experienced, and to emphasize the reality of transitions and transformation, the kind of molting that humans go through at different stages of life, but that the dominant culture doesn't acknowledge. I'd wanted to offer him the possibility that death, the death of an old self, is painful, but it isn't "wrong." It's not failing. I'd wanted to pose the idea that suffering is awful, but not necessarily "bad." And that he was allowed to seek a life that felt good to him, not just one that seemed "successful" or "productive." Perhaps the most important lesson for Conner was that if his body was miserable, distracted, uncomfortable, or bored, he was allowed to listen to it and inquire: "Why?" He didn't need to just shove those feelings away and cope, find substances to make it better, or try harder and harder to adapt to the very environment or relationships that were causing him pain.

"God. I am *so* glad I'm not graduating with a Comms degree." Conner cracked his knuckles again and laughed. "That would have been the degree for my whole life. It's just not me at all."

"You know that now."

"For real. I can't imagine what that would have set me up for. Like journalism? Advertising? That's not what I'm trying to do."

Conner had been particularly young when a disorienting inner crisis had hit him. But afterward, he'd had an opportunity to find what actually interested him before he got even further down a path that required gritting his teeth to stay on track. He now knew that it was never going to work, no matter how hard he'd tried.

"I'm looking forward to learning about the organs and all that," Conner told me. "I'm, like, actually looking forward to the biology labs."

Over the years, I have watched Quarterlifers move into

creative lives and begin to speak their truths in ways that astound me. This kind of wisdom and creativity is part of every aspect of development, but periods of integration invite a new kind of breakthrough. I am continually impressed by the ways my clients have defined these moments with incredible specificity, combining their own creative insights and skills with new technologies, old philosophies, and their own aesthetics to manifest lives and paths that I could never have conceived would bring them so much joy.

"I know college is gonna be really hard. I know being on campus with my teammates and not playing ball is going to feel weird. And I'm scared to see Eva," Conner shared with me in our final session. We were beginning to say goodbye. "But I think . . . I don't know. I'm excited about the possibility of being a doctor someday." He was almost luminous saying this.

If I'd compared this image of him with the man I'd first met in my waiting room, I'm not sure I would have believed they were the same person. I also knew that life would keep shifting and changing for Conner. Our work, and the integration of all he'd learned, was not a conclusion, but a new beginning. Conner was happy and he had tools now to understand his own individual life. That was a huge win and a tremendous new start. I felt genuinely proud of him as we said goodbye.

Feeling Whole

"How's being back at work?"

Mira made a face, her eyes wide and a bit frustrated. This

was her first week back at her law firm after her time away. She had just begun to enjoy her new schedule: getting up, going to a small studio almost every day and painting, sometimes struggling in front of a canvas, other times elated by what she created. We'd anticipated a bit of pain when she returned to work.

"There are so many office dynamics that I think I just blocked out before," Mira began.

"What have you noticed?"

"I don't know. It's like . . ." She paused. "It's like . . ." She paused again. "I think I can actually feel people's stress now. I used to just bury it all. But man, people are stressed over there!"

"It's pretty bad, huh?"

"It's really bad. It's like I fasted for three months and then started eating junk food right away. It's sort of awful. I don't know how long I'm going to be able to take it."

"What are you thinking?"

The fact that she knew she no longer wanted to be a lawyer still lingered. Revelations often take time to put into practice, but I did wonder how long Mira would be able to keep this up.

"I don't know yet, honestly. It's only been three days and all I can think is how I'd rather be home." Mira laughed at her newfound love of not working. "I never expected I'd be like this."

Mira no longer had difficulty conceiving of a different way to live. The fear of painting that had once consumed her and kept her frozen, like a fear of freedom for a long-caged animal, had finally melted. Her creative life no longer felt like an adversary. Her desire for her own life no longer felt like a threat.

"How's Mirabai doing with you being back at work?"

Mira thought about what I'd asked for a minute. This reference to her two conflicting selves had become a sort of shorthand between us, like a story we both knew well. We were familiar with the characters and their motivations and tracked them closely.

"I think she's okay? I mean, I think she kind of knows . . ." Mira sighed and paused. "I think she knows that this job has probably come to an end."

I raised my eyebrows.

"I know I can't do this much longer," Mira continued. "It's just become way too clear that it's not what I want anymore."

I nodded, comforted by Mira's clarity.

"Oh, bizarre . . ." Mira was looking up, thinking deeply.

"What's that?" I asked. "What's bizarre?"

She laughed. "I think I just saw Jennifer and Mirabai in the same place. Like . . . oh my god . . . are you sure this isn't dumb?"

"It's not dumb," I responded. "Something arose for you from the unconscious. Just witness it. What do you mean they were in the same place?"

"Like, I think these two sides of myself have always been sort of divided from each other, like in different universes or rooms inside of me . . . but now it's like they actually know each other."

Mira smacked herself lightly on the forehead and leaned

over her knees, head down. When she came back up, she was crying.

"What are you feeling?" I began slowly. Of course, I could tell something profound had just happened.

"I don't know. It's like . . ." Mira was no longer trying to control her tears. "It's like this weird, deep truth that what I've been doing is real."

"You're relieved," I offered.

"Yeah, that's it. Exactly. I feel relieved. Like deeply, deeply relieved." She took a breath, reflecting on her inner life. "It's like I'm not split and compartmentalized anymore."

This was the result of all of Mira's hard work to come into balance. The initial integration of her two disparate selves. She'd felt it deeply, and yet the inner experience of it can be hard to explain. To feel *whole* after feeling *split* is like feeling an absence of a headache or nausea; it's the sense of quiet and wellness where before there was persistent, gnawing discomfort. This is an experience that can be hard to explain to people who have never felt that discomfort before, never longed to Integrate with their other side, especially when the "wins" aren't external or easily observed.

Indeed, Mira was now *less* successful at work than she had been. She wasn't as much of an enthusiastic or devoted employee, and the security of a good salary no longer felt like motivation enough to stay at her firm. In certain ways, her life was also less secure than before we'd started working together. But internally, Mira felt more secure than ever. She knew who she was now and she knew how to connect her divergent parts, rather than silo them off in different realms.

She was stronger, clearer about her purpose, and no longer afraid that one side of herself was lying in wait to sabotage the other. That sense of inner security, then, provided deep validation. She wasn't haunted by her own life and afraid of a looming catastrophe she couldn't control. And, I learned, she was clarifying her own priorities more and more too.

"I think we're going to start trying to get pregnant," Mira began again, after a long silence.

"Oh yeah?" I exclaimed. "Tell me more."

"I think that's part of what all of this has been about for me. I know now that I want to be a mother more than anything, even though my own mom wanted something else for me." She sighed a little. "I just know now that I want to be at home painting and cooking, and hopefully raising a baby, much more than I want to be at the office all day long. I actually want a life more like my mother's, in the end. Or at least for now."

Mira's deeply held values had transformed—or emerged. She had discovered that the life she most wanted was contrary to what she'd been working toward for years. In many respects, it was contrary to what her mother had wanted for her daughter. But Mira had successfully steered a full life change without the collapse or crisis that she'd felt had been brewing inside of her. I was often impressed, and a little surprised, that her marriage had endured such a radical life shift, so soon after the wedding. Her husband understood the unresolved grief from her mother's death, and wanted her to have the space to process that. And as a lawyer himself, he also understood that while Mira was excellent at what she did, it wasn't what she wanted.

Mira looked out the window for a second and then back at me, wiping her nose with the crumpled tissue in her hand.

"Tom's said that I've been a lot happier lately." She laughed. "Well, he hasn't said it exactly, but I think I'm easier to be around now. He likes that I'm sharing more of my life with him."

"Does it feel different to you too?"

"Yeah. I think I'm paying a lot more attention to him than I used to too! And I've been really loving cooking too! Have I told you about that?"

"Just a little."

"Yeah. I've been cooking through my mother's folder of recipes and I've been having so much fun. I need to go to the Indian market to get the right spices and some frozen foods that aren't in other stores, and I've started to get to know a couple of the women who own those shops or run them." She smiled broadly. "It's been really nice."

It didn't happen right away, but Mira did get pregnant. They struggled through some fertility issues as well as a miscarriage before she felt secure enough to share the news of her pregnancy. In the meantime, she began to plan how to strategically leave work, while maintaining her healthcare and maternity leave. But by that point, those questions were entirely logistical. Mira was emotionally done with work and ready to enjoy being home, cooking, going to her studio to paint, and, most recently, learning how to reupholster old furniture. She wanted to begin preparing their home for a child. She didn't anticipate going back to work for a while after the baby was born, though she imagined she wasn't *entirely* done with being a lawyer. She was just allowing things to be open and uncertain, which was a huge change in itself. Mira was happy in an uncomplicated, unambivalent way.

Our last session came a few months before Mira gave birth. A couple months after her baby arrived, she sent me a photo of them both, and a note.

"This is really, really hard. I am so sleep-deprived, I can't believe how people do this. But I have also never felt clearer about who I am in my whole life. I honestly feel at peace with things in a way I never have before."

Reaping the Rewards

"This editor I've been working with asked me if she could submit one of my stories to a competition online," Danny told me one afternoon. "She thinks my story might have a good shot."

"No way!" I exclaimed. I congratulated him on this vote of confidence from someone I knew he deeply respected.

"She also thinks I should go to graduate school," Danny continued, grimacing a bit. "She thinks it might help me finish my collection."

I'd read one of Danny's stories, a sort of post-apocalyptic, sci-fi story of a young man coming of age in Cuba. I told him that I hadn't known what to expect but that I was deeply impressed by how beautiful it was.

Danny worked hard over the next few months on a tight deadline to get several applications out to some highly respected writing programs. Within another six months, he'd been accepted to several and received scholarships to two. Then Danny won the short story competition that he'd submitted to as well. The delight of this unfolding recognition of his work was infectious. He was proud and beaming, and each time he arrived with a new piece of news, I was beaming too. It would have been hard to conceive of this steadily un-folding success just a few years prior when we'd met.

And yet, his writing career wasn't the only thing unfold-ing. Almost simultaneously, there was another major change.

"What's going on?" I looked almost skeptically at Danny one day after he'd been unusually silent at the start of our session. I couldn't tell if things were terrible or wonderful, but he seemed to be guarding a secret.

"I met someone," Danny began, blushing.

"Oh! You're happy!" I was relieved. "You met someone?"

He nodded.

"Do you want to tell me more?"

Danny shrugged, coy. He took his time, perhaps afraid that sharing would break some sort of spell, but also eager to tell me everything.

"She's pretty cool . . ." Danny smiled, bashfully.

"Where did you meet?"

"She's in my Saturday yoga class. I've had a crush on her for a long time." Danny looked full of fear and delight. He crossed one leg over the other. "She's awesome."

Danny had been looking much stronger and far less le-thargic to me over the last many months. The difference was stark: He stood up straighter and no longer appeared de-feated by life. There was a resilience and fortitude about him that hadn't been there before. And now it was easy to see how smitten Danny was by the half-glazed look in his eyes.

Danny couldn't believe his luck. This girl liked him. She liked him even though she'd seen him move in yoga class, which Danny found impossible to believe. He couldn't imagine that someone would want his body. That he might be appealing to another person. That he could like her and that she could like him back. This, in itself, was exciting, and healing.

"She's in school for physical therapy." Danny raised his eyebrows at me, impressed and delighted. "It seems like a good opposite for my nature, I think." The physicality, he meant, to his own contemplative, writerly self. Someone, perhaps, to keep modeling for him what embodied health could look like.

Danny had grown through the consistent, reliable relationship with me, a core component of most therapy. Comfort. Attachment. Mirroring. But when Danny started this romantic relationship, things improved further. He began to grow and mature in new ways through the joy of a safe, committed, nonjudgmental partnership with a person who also knew her own boundaries and needs. They were able to love each other, and also set limits with each other. And Danny began to journey through entirely new territory sexually too. He had needed the experience of exploring his own emotional life and sexual power safely, without feeling ashamed of his body or feeling dominating toward a woman he respected. In this relationship, he was able to allow desire to emerge organically, and learned to share his own vulnerabilities and fears too.

Over the coming weeks and months, Danny and his girlfriend went on short trips around the state and regular hikes out into the wilderness. They ate well together. They slept well. Danny felt companionship without feeling exhausted, and for the first time in years, he had an enduring physical experience of relaxation and joy.

"I'm broke now from everything we've been doing. Completely broke. But damn," Danny exclaimed.

"Worth it?"

"Oh yeah. No question."

Danny had a swagger about him now.

"I think I've always felt like I was underwater," he told me one day, reflecting on the changes. "Or stranded out in the ocean."

"Like you were drowning?"

"Yeah, like I was drowning or just, totally lost and adrift. I don't feel like that anymore."

"No? What does it feel like now?" I asked.

"It feels like, even if I'm out in the water, I have a strong tether to get back with, or a platform to stand on. I don't have this desperate sense that I'm lost or going to drown."

I flashed back to the months when I first met Danny, when he'd appeared so utterly depleted. It wouldn't have been a stretch to imagine him literally waterlogged and panicking. I loved this image that he was reflecting now: safety within the water, a way to get back to land.

Danny stayed in therapy with me until he left for his MFA program. We'd worked together for nearly four years by that point—an enduring mentorship/therapeutic relationship that is very common, though it's not celebrated by insurance companies, nor by a culture that likes "quick fixes." By the time Danny left for school, his life was no longer just about surviving. He no longer wanted to brush off existence like an annoying affliction. Daily life still contained bouts of depression and anxiety, to be sure. He worried about countless social issues, climate change, and about his friends in pain. He still struggled with energy and self-care. But in the core of himself, Danny felt a foundational sense of security. He felt that his life could hold space for safety and mystery too. Danny was aware that new struggles and disappointments would arise, but he also felt able to genuinely celebrate being in the world, with all the world had to offer.

Blossoming

"I looked into these women's business classes in town," Grace shared, clearly excited and a little nervous.

"Oh yeah? What classes?"

"They're oriented for women who are thinking about building a small business. More on budgeting and bookkeeping, but also stuff like where to get loans and how to manage inventory. All sorts of stuff."

"Oh, how cool."

"Yeah. It just seems like a good thing for me to do, you know? I've been really enjoying managing my money better." Grace laughed out loud. "Is that silly? That I'm enjoying 'managing my money'?" She asked in a fake fancy voice, waggling her shoulders as she spoke.

"Do you think it's silly?"

"No, I like it. I've been giving my mom advice on her money too. We looked at her credit card rates together and, mercy! She needed help with that." Grace shook her head and looked at the ground. "I really can't even believe it."

"That bad, huh?"

"It's so bad. No wonder she's been stressed out my whole life! I mean, let's be honest, it's been for a million reasons, but that's one of them."

"So, you two are talking more these days too?"

"A little more."

"How's it been?"

"She said she'd go to a family therapist with me, a few times, if I visit."

"Wow. I'm surprised, I guess." Based on her characterization of her mother, that was not an offer I would have expected. "Do you think you'll do it?"

"I'd like to." Grace nodded a bit. "We need it. I think it could help her a lot too."

Grace was twenty-six now. She was still growing, but a lot had changed. She'd started a new job at a flower store in her neighborhood some months after she began tackling her finances. She'd stepped into the desire to get more serious about her career, and knew she needed to make more money. The flower shop paid only two more dollars an hour than she had made serving, but it made a big difference for Grace, and it was more aligned with her interests. She loved her co-workers and loved being around the plants all day long. Things were distinctly more stable and energizing for her, and meaningful too.

"Ultimately, I want to open my own flower cart," Grace explained. "That's the business plan I'm going to work on."

"A cart? Like a food truck?"

"Yeah, like I want to convert a little bus. I've been searching for them online. And I'm talking with people who own food trucks about some of the requirements for parking and licensing and all."

A whole plan for Grace's future was emerging. She was developing faith in her capacity to create something and stand on her own. She'd learned a lot about herself socially and romantically too.

It had been a couple of years since Grace had moved into her own apartment. She'd been dating and working on the clear communication and boundary-setting that dating can engender. She was slowly shifting her sense of her own limits, neither enmeshed and reliant on one person nor entirely available to her group of friends like a living blood bank, offering up her veins to anyone who needed her energy, attention, or wise counsel. Grace had begun to be able to hear what her body and feelings were saying. She'd learned to subtly notice what *she* needed, rather than always leaning into the needs of others in order to avoid rejection. She'd learned to say no—or, at least, she was practicing. And she'd also learned how much alone time she actually required.

"I've been loving being alone lately so, so much," she'd expressed, almost beaming.

"Are you starting to think you might actually be an introvert?" I smiled.

"Ha!" Grace laughed. "Maybe?"

"I think sometimes if we don't get enough alone time, that cycle of extroversion can be more like mania than actual energizing social time," I offered. "Like we can think we're super social and we're actually just half-crazed and exhausted."

Grace raised her eyebrows. "Oh my god. Totally! That makes so much sense. I really don't feel manic the way I used to." She was thinking it through. "I don't think I used to ever want to be alone because, like, I just always thought it was so scary. But I seriously really crave it now." Grace stretched her legs out in front of her. "I think that's also part of why I'm excited about the business courses. I want to have something to study and really focus on at home."

Grace had started to discover that with enough alone time, she could enter the world without a sense of imminent overwhelm. These days, she felt more regulated, less likely to sputter out and dissolve.

Bit by bit, all of Grace's work had begun to flower like a garden thoughtfully planted and tended. She was Integrating what she'd learned and composting the rest. More and more, her past traumas were just fertilizer for her future.

At the end of our last session, Grace asked me rhetorically, "Why does no one ever teach you these things?"

"What do you mean?" I asked.

"Just all this stuff. Like, how to be human! No one ever teaches you how to be human!"

I shrugged. "I don't know, honestly," I commiserated with her. "There's so little emotional and psychological guidance for people your age—for anyone really!"

"Seriously! I'm actually looking forward to this next phase of things," Grace shared. "Life feels like an adventure now! That sounds so corny. But I really don't feel like I'm just trying to stay alive. I think that's how I used to be, just all the time. Trying to survive."

I nodded. "I think so too. And you were doing a good job at it."

"Yeah, but it's like I'm actually looking forward to things now. To challenges. To see what I can do next."

I raised my eyebrows at her in one last teasing, joyful expression of shock. I felt so impressed by the woman in front of me.

"I'm really happy to hear it," I told her.

Conclusion

I t's important for books like these to expand our sense of what is possible—if not through happy resolutions, at least by illuminating the path ahead. When we're feeling lost or are suffering, we need genuine hope for a radically different future. We need stories of transformation in order to believe that there's a way out of pain, and a way forward. When I was struggling to find my own path in Quarterlife, working joyless jobs, stressed about money and the state of the world and my future, I needed to know that there was at least a possibility for a different life. Stories of Quarterlifers, true or mythic, with a sense of joy and potential in their endings, helped me enormously. In this book, I wanted to show the same. I now know that a much better future is possible for Quarterlifers.

Of course, this is not "the end" of the stories of Mira, Conner, Grace, or Danny. I anticipate that each of them has many decades of life ahead, and life will continue to provide them with challenges, as well as surprising gifts. But the goal—my hope—is that the growth and tools gained through the conscious work to Separate from their pasts, Listen to themselves, Build their lives in Quarterlife, and Integrate stability and meaning will help them navigate the inner and outer storms. These same pillars and points of focus can be returned to over and over again to regain orientation and enhance a sense of balance.

And yet, it must be said stories with hopeful endings are not the only ones. I can't help but fear that such clear resolutions may become a source of shame for readers who feel that their progress is stalled or "taking too long." Know this too: In addition to the extraordinary changes I have witnessed, I have also struggled with some clients for years to gain true insight into their suffering or how to help them. Maybe it's an addiction that they can't kick, a harmful belief system that they can't let go of, an abusive relationship that's holding on like a vise, a neurodivergence with which I'm unfamiliar, or a medication that needs to be prescribed, adjusted, or removed. I'm aware of and humbled by all these possibilities when a client is stuck in their healing and growth in ways that defy their—and my—understanding.

It's worth emphasizing that central to many of these issues around Quarterlifers being "stuck" is a history of trauma, in all shapes and sizes. Traumatized Quarterlifers are everywhere. Even when a person is spared trauma, a lifetime in school with an emphasis on left-brain learning and high-stress competition, combined with a regular if not constant relationship to digital devices, can dissociate a person from their physical body, as well as any experience of their inner life and imagination. This overly linear, logical, and two-dimensional world leaves Quarterlifers dissociated. Trauma researcher and psychologist Peter Levine makes the same point: "It is not just acutely traumatized individuals who are disembodied; most Westerners share a less dramatic but still impairing disconnection from their inner sensate compasses." We need those inner compasses to find our way.

One of my great hopes for the future of mental healthcare and for Quarterlife therapy is an increased emphasis on embodied, trauma-informed care. This means more trauma-informed clinicians, but also the resources to pay for treatment. It may mean creating care centers where Quarterlifers could go on retreat, able to spend periods of time—cost free—to heal, recuperate, and find relief from symptoms that threaten their lives and keep them from thriving. Despite being a trauma-informed therapist myself, there are many times when I wish I could easily refer a client to such a retreat center where they would receive top-level care from a team of trained practitioners who specialize in healing psychological trauma with the body in mind—and that such care would be paid for fully by insurance. In my fantasy, these are beautiful places, like old monasteries, with abundant nature, silence, and nutritious food. This kind of care could save lives, keep people out of drug rehab, jail, and homelessness, prevent physical illnesses and suicide attempts, and interrupt the cycles of relational abuse that we know can stem from past hurt. Normalizing periods of long-term retreat, and improving accessible, trauma-informed care should be a national priority.

But when I think about the future of Quarterlife psychotherapy, high-level, funded trauma treatment is just the beginning. I know that when a Quarterlifer is "stuck," "failing to launch," or "failing to thrive," there may also be one of the myriad aspects of structural inequity at play.

One of the great difficulties of being a therapist is regularly encountering the effects of social inequality and injustice in my office, without the scope or power to alter things, economically or otherwise, for my clients—or for the clients who never make it through my door. There are issues that I can handle as a therapist, and there are issues that I cannot.

I cannot adjust the skyrocketing cost of higher education and ballooning student loans that leave many Quarterlifers unable to pull themselves out of debt despite having "done everything right"—and that prevent many other Quarterlifers from ever attending college or pursuing an advanced degree. I cannot address the similarly out of control cost of housing and the growing discrepancy between wages and the cost of living.

I cannot solve the fact that many of my clients do not have health insurance to cover psychotherapy, or struggle to cover the high deductibles or co-pays that would allow them to see me. I alone cannot carry a full psychotherapy practice of sliding-scale rates or stay in-network with the dizzying number of insurance companies, most of which undervalue mental healthcare and pay well below the average national rates for mental health treatment.

I cannot ensure that Quarterlifers graduate from high school with at least the basics of financial literacy, the foundations of cooking and nutrition, an introduction to healthy communication, boundary setting, and the dangers of abuse in dating, as well as some fundamentals around healthcare and self-care that could quickly improve quality of life if not save lives.

I cannot help those Quarterlifers who are struggling with immigration bureaucracy in this country, or in war zones, refugee camps, and border towns around the world to gain the freedom to pursue their dreams that should be a basic human right.

I cannot guarantee that any Quarterlifer who becomes pregnant is able to choose for themselves what to do with their body and future.

I cannot protect Quarterlifers from gun violence in their neighborhoods and schools.

I cannot stop the climate crisis that threatens their future livelihoods.

I could go on and on.

While my work is to focus on the psychology of Quarterlife, there is always, always another aspect on my mind: the refusal to care about this time of life as a social justice issue. For countless Quarterlifers in our communities and around the world, structural issues that are completely outside of their control block opportunities for living free and full lives, no matter how hard they may work to change things.

While society delights in obsessing over the love lives and celebrity of countless Quarterlife musicians, athletes, and actors, there is a similar obsession with deriding their actual well-being, criticizing every misstep, and mocking every genuine mental health concern. This same attitude filters down into families and communities. Arguably, Quarterlife success is a primary focus of culture from living rooms to Hollywood to the Olympics, and yet lamenting or jeering the inability to always perform perfectly, for one reason or another, is also practically a national pastime.

What if we took a different approach?

What if supporting Quarterlife, just as we are making forays into supporting early childhood development and end-of-life care, could become a national priority?

I too was once steeped in the cultural disregard for early adulthood. I too thought my curiosity was of little import, and had to battle aside countless inner demons imploring me to focus on "the more important issues" that had once held my exclusive attention. But there was a feeling that was unrelenting, a need to understand this strange, unappreciated terrain of psychology that wouldn't leave me and that sat on my shoulders like a dead weight, never relaxing or letting go until I embraced the curiosity with my whole body. What I've learned is that when we talk about Quarterlife development, we are really talking about the development of mature citizens, community members, partners, and parents. We are talking about the shepherding of human growth and the choice for a society to host the maturation of healthy humans—or not. To disregard this emphasis with the eyerolls and commentary too often lobbed against people in Quarterlife because of long-standing projections onto this age group is to disregard opportunities for a more sane society. A society in which our growing citizens are well educated, well-fed, housed, and given access to the mental and physical healthcare that they need. A society in which Quarterlifers, as they build their independent lives, feel free to make their own decisions, and have insight into how to create loving, conscious relationships, including raising their own children—should they choose to have them—with love and attention, the resources to support them, and the healthy boundaries needed, someday, to also let them go.

Every population that has brought grievances before governments and dominant cultures has initially—and for a long time thereafter—found resistance, ridicule, and rejection. In the histories of activism and change, various age groups have lobbied for protections and attention, or others have done so on their behalf. Child labor was once viewed as acceptable. Guaranteed social security benefits and Medicare for the elderly were once just ideas. Free public education for kindergarten through high school was also once just a dream.

Similarly, the notion that the structural and social obstacles affecting Quarterlifers are areas of collective concern requiring legislation, protections, and funding may initially seem absurd to some, or hard to comprehend. And yet, from economic issues such as student loan forgiveness and accessibility of first-time home ownership, to broader issues such as military requirement, policing in Black and brown communities, the disappearance and murders of Native women, the murders of trans women, the relentless attacks on reproductive rights, and rates of homelessness in the LGBTQIA+ community, it is *Quarterlifers who are primarily affected.*

Whether it be in regard to economic opportunities— a key component of forging an independent life—or embodied freedom and safety, the societal issues afflicting Quarterlifers today hamper growth for many, and create obstacles enough for a torture chamber for others.

It bears mentioning that we are recently emerging (I hope?) from a global pandemic that affected the lives of Quarterlifers in dramatic and sometimes devastating ways. Many of my clients found initial relief in the pandemic, in the ability to take a break from relentless workdays, financial stress, and social obligations for the first time in their lives, while receiving small unemployment checks to help pay for necessities. Many used this time in remarkable ways to do deep psychological work that had been impossible while juggling everything else. With some rest from the hustle of existence, they transformed their lives. But other clients of mine and Quarterlifers everywhere also experienced relentless, toxic stress trying to maintain childcare, eldercare, financial survival, their own healthcare, online classes, extreme isolation, and on. Countless Quarterlifers saw job and school opportunities disappear in front of their eyes. On incredibly short notice, they abandoned their dorm rooms, still filled with all their things, for months and months, and graduated virtually, unable to hug their friends or properly say goodbye.

Gratefully, other writers have tackled all these various topics affecting Quarterlifers in numerous articles and books. Some commentators are addressing ways that people in this age group were affected by the pandemic and are affected by climate change, immigration policies, incarceration rates, and reproductive healthcare. Others are attending to the generational disparities in access to first-time home ownership and higher education—research in which the use of generational names like "boomers" versus "millennials" can become truly relevant and helpful. (See Jill Filipovic's book *OK Boomer, Let's Talk* for an excellent breakdown on this.) But, in general, because of the lack of a single name for this time of life—or even the struggle to see it *as a stage of life*—writers and activists have yet to be unified around the potential value of a nation's Quarterlifers having the rights and supports necessary to build independent lives and flourish.

I dream of a culture at-large that provides true guidance and financial assistance for struggling Quarterlifers, not guns on every corner, jail at every crisis, or substances for every grief. My hope is not to create a gilded slide from adolescence to midlife (I can already hear the jaded critiques to my suggestion). To be alive is to be embodied. To be embodied is to struggle and thrive and struggle and thrive. This inherent oscillation is our birthright. Our charter is to learn how to ride the changes, become our fullest selves, create, and love. I am clear that life's complications and even suffering—as many theologians, philosophers, and psychologists before me have expressed—are themselves core to development, to maturity, and to gaining a deeply rooted sense of meaning in life. James Baldwin wrote, "People who cannot suffer can never grow up, can never discover who they are." But, as Baldwin also spent his life asserting, the dominant society can and must do better to care for every one of its citizens.

Quarterlife really does not have to be *this* hard.

If the pursuit of stability and meaning in Quarterlife is seen as necessary to normal human development and, therefore, is recognized as a social justice issue, we can bring under one roof countless problems against which Quarterlifers are struggling—and to which they're frequently succumbing. We can, collectively, make the first part of adulthood less riddled with traps, tricks, and quicksand. The result would be less individual suffering, to be sure—which should be motivation enough. But it would also lead to a fundamentally healthier culture. When our citizens and community members begin their adult lives with greater opportunity and orientation, and with a feeling that *they are cared for as vital members of society,* our entire social fabric improves. We needn't continue the generations-long hazing and admonishment: "*I* figured it out. Why can't you?"

As timeless as this journey is, the path was never easy. There is, unfortunately perhaps, no checklist for surviving and thriving in Quarterlife. There is only the journey of our individual lives, a personal responsibility and personal joy of self-discovery and healing, a pursuit that society can support in myriad ways, or can interrupt and sabotage. We can do better. For countless Quarterlifers, the path can be easier than it is. It can be filled with more love, empathy, safety, and tangible support. I can only hope that this book will offer some outline of what is required to walk the deeply psychological path of Quarterlife and find, in the end, an embodied, alive experience of one's singular life, one's truth, and hopefully, the entwined, integrated experience of structure and purpose, of stability and meaning too.

Acknowledgments

Without my clients, this book would be just theory. I am eternally grateful to them for teaching me so much over the years and for helping me to refine my understanding of Quarterlife. I am similarly indebted to my many therapists, healers, and teachers who, throughout my Quarterlife years, helped me to survive and find my path.

I've been envisioning and writing this book, in one form or another, for more than a decade. I spent years on research, a master's thesis, and various articles before it finally came to fruition. Thank you to the board at *Psychological Perspectives* who accepted a piece on the Jungian view of the "first half of life" and saw in it the potential for a book. I'm grateful to Robert Hinshaw, who believed in that article, provided early edits, and helped to shepherd its publication. Thank you to Elise Loehnen and Kiki Koroshetz, who published a later article of mine in *Goop*. Within a week of that piece being published, my soon-to-be agent, David McCormick, reached out to me. David taught me the ropes and made sure a proposal got into the right hands. And it did. I could not be more grateful to David and to Julie Grau, my original editor at Random House who acquired this book on proposal. My appreciation for their belief in this book is beyond words.

This book had its own timeline. Thank you to Caitlin McKenna, my second editor at Random House, for taking on an orphaned book, and for being a gatekeeper on earlier, poorly structured, not good drafts. And special thanks to my third and final editor, Emma Caruso, who took over when Caitlin went on maternity leave and has since, over several years, supported the shaping of this book with remarkable focus. The book I'd initially envisioned matured with Emma's dedication, questions, insights, and devotion.

Thank you to Liz Carbonell, my extraordinary copy editor, and my two authenticity readers, Mya Alexice and Meenakshi Venkat, who all provided thoughtful fine-tuning. I'm grateful to Victoria Wong for the beautiful layout of this book, and to all the people at Random House who have been involved in the editing, design, layout, marketing, and project management whose names I do not know. I am grateful to my fact-checker, Julie Tate, who was available on short notice to check the book and saved me from several mostly small but embarrassing mistakes. I'm so very thankful to Nina Bunjevac for the remarkable illustrations in these pages, and for her belief in this project.

In the midst of the publication journey, there was a personal one. I am grateful to Kirsten Collins, who was there for my Quarterlife breakdowns and yet, somehow, has believed in my career and this book with incredible sincerity from day one. To Holly Herrera, who has been a remarkably stalwart friend since we met as college roommates and was my most on-call therapist-friend for years (and years). I'm grateful to Evan Schneider and Judith Edwards, who have been around for this journey from proposal through early drafts and many a supportive conversation. Thank you to Rebecca Hyman, who helped me work through sticky parts of the theory in this book, and who then offered detailed notes on a near-final draft to make it better. I'm grateful to Michelle Ruiz Keil, who read a very early draft and then a much later draft and helped with some clutch improvements when I needed them most. Thank you to Jill Filipovic, who offered some very important feedback on where to cut and what to keep and has been nothing but supportive. And to Sara Guest, John Brehm, Kwame Scruggs, Lauren Gniazdowski, Sam Alexander, Lindsay Ratowsky, Ayana Jamieson, and other friends, family, and colleagues along the way: thank you.

I would be lost without my Salome Institute community, in particular Carol Ferris and Kelley Swenson and my long-time students, the Salomates. Robin Mesch and Scott Hanley hosted my Salome salons in their living room for two years and believed in me fiercely from the jump. Your friendship and repeated, tangible help have meant the world.

Words cannot express my gratitude to my mother, Anita Doyle, who introduced me to Jung's work and the world of dreams, and who sent me off to college with a copy of *The I Ching*. At the same time, my father, Ira Byock, showed me what life as a clinician-writer-activist-professional could look like. Your mutual positive influence on my life and career can't be quantified. Thank you to my stepmother, Yvonne

Corbeil, who—along with my mom and dad—read the final draft of this book with incisive comments and enthusiasm and has been supportive at every step. I'm so grateful.

Thank you to Aunt Molly, for her endless celebration of me and for her interest in attending my classes. Thank you to my sister and brother-in-law, Lila Byock and Sam Shaw, for their celebration of this book, help with questions along the way, and the ultimately convincing conversation to change some characters' names. (Thanks, Li.)

And finally, my endless gratitude to Jay, who believed in this book from the very beginning and has since talked with me about it in detail in countless conversations, offered brilliant edits on drafts over and over again, and provided emotional support. For all this, but not just for this, I could not love you more.

ABOUT THE AUTHOR

SATYA DOYLE BYOCK is a licensed psychotherapist, writer, and the director of The Salome Institute of Jungian Studies. Her work is informed by analytical psychology, history, and social justice advocacy. She lives in Portland.

satyabyock.com

ABOUT THE TYPE

This book was set in Sabon, a typeface designed by the well-known German typographer Jan Tschichold (1902–74). Sabon's design is based upon the original letter forms of sixteenth-century French type designer Claude Garamond and was created specifically to be used for three sources: foundry type for hand composition, Linotype, and Monotype. Tschichold named his typeface for the famous Frankfurt typefounder Jacques Sabon (c. 1520–80).